SKIING WITH DOSTOYEVSKY

New & Selected Poems

\\

ALSO BY DAVID AXELROD

//

POETRY

Years Beyond the River
The Open Hand
Folly
What Next, Old Knife?
Departing by a Broken Gate
The Cartographer's Melancholy
The Chronicles of the Withering State
The Kingdom at Hand
Jerusalem of Grass

ESSAYS

The Eclipse I Call Father: Essays on Absence
Troubled Intimacies

EDITOR

Sensational Nightingales:
Collected Poems of Walter Pavlich

SKIING WITH DOSTOYEVSKY

New & Selected Poems

DAVID AXELROD

LynxHousePress

FIRST EDITION

Cover Art: *Icebergs Under Cloudy Skies*, Frederic Edwin Church, gift of Louis P. Church (June or July 1859) and courtesy of Cooper Hewitt, Smithsonian Design Museum
Author Photo: Jodi Varon
Designed by Lauren Hohle

LYNX HOUSE PRESS books are distributed by the WSU Press, Cooper Publications Building, PO Box 645910, Pullman, WA 99164-5910
LIBRARY OF CONGRESS CATALOGING-IN-PUBLICATION DATA is available from the Library of Congress.
ISBN 978-0-89924-198-2

CONTENTS

\\

Skiing with Dostoyevsky

New Poems

Waking in the Capital :: 14
A Plea to Strangers :: 15
Simplicissimus :: 16
A Letter to His Ex from Fishtown :: 17
Hillel's Song of Acknowledgement :: 18
When the Middle Game Is Over :: 19
From the End of Winter :: 21
To the Angel of Forgetting :: 22
A Blank Day :: 23
Peripheries :: 24
And Hurrying to Catch the 43 :: 26
Whiskey & Crank :: 27
Firasah :: 28
Signal Fires :: 29
The Spring Classics :: 30
Real Good :: 32
A Toast on Midsummer's Eve :: 33
A Toast to Heavenly Bodies :: 34
Below Medicine Bow Peak :: 35
How Do I Remember Them? :: 36
In the Land of 1,000 Dances :: 37
Black Walnuts :: 39
The Woe There Is in Marriage :: 40
Trespasses :: 41
Along the Troll-Løypa :: 43

Einfühlung :: 44
Song of Extinctions :: 45
Miserere :: 46
First Night Out Since You Died :: 47
Tzadik Moshe :: 48
The Readiness Is All :: 49
Hillel's Parable of Burdens :: 50

Jerusalem of Grass
1992

Allegiances :: 54
Bainbridge Dairy :: 56
A Friend Phones from New York City :: 57
In Tongues :: 59
Kaddish :: 61
Across the Great Divide :: 62
Regarding a Nude on Diamond Mountain :: 64

The Kingdom at Hand
1993

"An older man wants to know if my generation..." :: 68
"It's taken three days of wandering..." :: 70
"In June sunlight below snowbanks..." :: 72
"One autumn, I traced this glacier-vein..." :: 75
"Persistent southwesterly winds shove dunes..." :: 76
"Sitting cross-legged in red volcanic ash..." :: 80

Chronicles of the Withering State
2004

A Minor Contemporary :: 84
The Consolations of Reverend Malthus :: 85
November 1989 :: 86
From the Anthology of the Last Republic (I) :: 87
From the Anthology of the Last Republic (II) (a fragment) :: 88
Of Attack :: 89
From the Anthology of the Last Republic (III) (a fragment) :: 90
Romantic Ode :: 91

A Pedagogic Parable :: 92
Whatever Happened to Our Old Revolution :: 93
Crooked Light :: 94

The Cartographer's Melancholy
2005

Tiled Mosaic :: 96
From the Book of Esther :: 100
An Offering :: 102
Fest-Spiel Weise :: 103
Tekmerion :: 104
The Cartographer's Melancholy :: 106
Gnosis :: 108
Of Water :: 110

Departing by a Broken Gate
2010

To the Morning Star :: 112
Another Metaphysical Error :: 113
Earthstar :: 115
Unifying Theory :: 116
On Finding a Friend Drunk at Lost Lake :: 117
After :: 118
The Morning Chorus :: 119
Georgic for My Friends Who Never Find Any :: 120
Behold–This Compost! :: 122
Departing By a Broken Gate :: 123

What Next, Old Knife?
2012

After Harvest :: 126
My Nationality [Redacted] :: 127
Swallow It :: 128
We're Not Good at This :: 130
In the Space of an Hour :: 133
I Missed My Parents Today :: 135
Yom Kippur in Stuttgart :: 136

Crossing Synagogenplatz :: 137
On Ebenalp :: 139
Carved from the Pit of a Date :: 143
Word Over All, Beautiful as Sky :: 145

Folly
2014

Theater of the Absurd :: 148
What Is Tenderness Anyway? :: 149
My Boulder Isn't :: 150
Listening to Shostakovich :: 151
A Colleague of Ours at the Institute :: 154
After Re-Reading *The Records of a Weather-exposed Skeleton* :: 155
Tithe :: 157
After a Fast, In a Field of Germinated Wheat :: 158

The Open Hand
2017

Dedication :: 160
Dream at the Jaffa Gate :: 162
In the Church of the Holy Sepulcher :: 163
Kinnahora :: 164
Trying to Grasp It :: 165
The Happiest Day :: 166
The Disciple :: 168
On Counting to Infinity :: 170
St. Jerome Rides the T :: 172
At Yad Vashem :: 173
Kaddish for Nicholas Meer :: 174
The Private Life of Debris :: 176
Julafton :: 178
Lines Composed on the Jaffa Road :: 180
What Simonetta Said :: 182

Years Beyond the River
2021

Balk :: 186
At the Wellhead :: 188

The Music Our Son Dreamed Of :: 189
Apostles of Imminence :: 191
As the Mountain Dreamed It :: 193
Late August in the Okanagan :: 195
A Message Passed Between Twilights :: 197
From *The Field Guide to North American Monkeys* :: 199
The North American Sorrow Monkey :: 200
From Late January :: 202
Crossing into the Deep North :: 203
We're Standing on the Green Line :: 204
At Nine-Geese-Cross-the-Sun :: 205
Lastness :: 206

Acknowledgments

SKIING WITH DOSTOYEVSKY

Dostoyevsky skis past you on a long, steep uphill called "The Meat Grinder," kicking straight up glazed tracks. So you have to ask, "Fyodorovitch, what makes you ski so strong?" And as he works the hill ahead of you into the forest, you think you hear him growl under his breath, "Idiot!" Compelled by this to stay close, you ski right up onto his heels, clipping the tails of his skis just to annoy him and ask, quoting him his own words, "You mean, 'simple ingratitude'?" He doesn't answer, but just goes on remorselessly into birch-covered hills. Already 25 kilometers into the race, your mind is off course, consumed by doubts about this ordeal, sickened by how far down inside you're expected to mine this black seam of negation. *It's absurd*, you think, *I don't care anymore. Piss on this. I give up.* Despite the drool and snot frozen on your beard, the blur before your eyes, at 48 kilometers strangers along the race course cry out, "Heia, heia! Hup, hup, hup!" their voices cheerful as devils. There's no disguising how this is turning out, nor the thousands of miserable lifetimes you've lived before this one, things always going awry. But Dostoyevsky–he's the most perverse bastard out here. One-hundred-eighty years old, give or take, and he's skiing no worse today than he did a century ago, refusing to concede time to anybody, least of all to Time. When you cross the finish line, he's waiting to console losers like you. But when you offer your hand, he seizes you, pulls you chest to chest, so you can smell the pickles on his breath, see the silver flecks of herring between his teeth. "Listen to me Duvy, listen close," he says, patting your cheek. "We learn to live between torment and the hope for mercy, though mercy never comes."

New Poems

//

Becoming foreign. To yourself and others.
So that's what a transition looks like.

–Jenny Erpenbeck

WAKING IN THE CAPITAL

At the speeds we travel
and given the shape of things
as we roar away, who can say
what strayed into
our right of way, whose wings,
whose eyes and astonishment
flared in our headlights?
The furnace whooshes awake,
clunks off again
and we doze until the mezzo
comes on the radio
singing, *Mein Gott,*
wenn kommt das Schöne
and we rise into our lives again.

A PLEA TO STRANGERS

The Enlightenment catches fire
and we sometimes let it burn to embers
at dusk, but it's been dusk for years
and now sunset shoves aside clouds
and ignites the flag on the Capitol dome,
its flames tethered to a spire,
whipped by wind. Grief weeps
on the shoulder of her sister History
and butchers shovel carts full of offal
into the municipal wells. I've unlatched
the Dung Gate and thrown it wide–Come,
fetch a bucket and fill it from the river,
come, maimed thief, swineherd's daughter,
all who are driven from the rural place
you can't return to, come, souls-in-waiting
from regions of rubble and feral dogs,
run the gauntlet of gibbets and jeering mob,
come, join the bucket brigade.

SIMPLICISSIMUS

Wet lumps huddle in doorways
and I take just a quick peek as I pass,
a little sip of the war's nitty-gritty.
The sky is so low and gray here,
it forces us to bend down so as not to
bump our heads against dreariness winter sends.
Add the roar of falls, a holiness
to the city's dispossessed tribes–
far off and persistent above traffic noise.
The river's laced with plumes of cyanide
from played-out silver mines
in foothills upstream, *from whence*,
my namesake, the warrior-king
and psalmodist, in a rare mood of social justice,
promised *help doth come*.
But if I cast mine eyes unto those hills,
help doth not come, only a street preacher
from the flophouse for women with children,
who hands me a soggy handbill and asks,
"Is it normal to feel this way?"
Good Lord, I wonder? When will mercy
crack the riddle-me-this and riddle-me-that?
"Hope begins here," the signboard
above the doorway reads, "No vacancy."

LETTER TO HIS EX FROM FISHTOWN

What you heard
and what I want you, please
to keep from our daughter, is true–
they ran me out of Spokane
like a fox, my pride docked and nailed to the door.

Fishtown too is the same
as thirty years ago when we arrived,
the two of us almost strangers then
as now–a contingency of planks and tin
salvaged from the cannery,
my shack's lashed to creosote pilings.

And it's true, I still haven't learned
how to keep my balance
on boardwalks slicked by rain. At dawn,
I zigzag through alders and–welcome
face smeared in mud,
soiled knees and seat of my pants.

When the tide's out,
eelgrass meadows lie flat and reek of muck.
And out on the bay,
fishermen hoist crab pots hand over fist.
When they flop the traps over,
shells clack on the riveted ribs of their skiffs.

That's the sound I listen for,
the crabs going into a frenzy
on their backs, dismayed,
full of spite, trying to right themselves
and climb for the gunwales.

HILLEL'S SONG OF ACKNOWLEDGEMENT

I piloted my little biplane
whose propeller puttered ahead of me
from the enthrallments of Babylon
to the Second Temple,
the revolutions of '48, and once,
from the Pale of Settlement,
Bubbe waved as I flew over,
cheering me on from the garden gate.
Below the wings, a light breeze
stirred the einkorn, rutted tracks
guided the way from fields
to market towns to Vilna and a ghetto
people escaped through sewers.

And wherever I landed my plane,
always the same question they asked
and neither naked nor clothed,
I replied—after the hell of each other,
if ocean is mercy,
if it's limitless and rising
(as we know it is!)
how much peril will we bear
before saltwater breaches
the seawalls shielding us from
a future whose partisans
it's already too late to join
in the forests we fled to before.

WHEN THE MIDDLE GAME IS OVER

Your children drive away and the river runs dry.
Everyone in town is watching, everyone
ready and willing as the cop next door
who told you once he'd shot a child
whose father everyone knew
beat the boy for years, before the kid
took the stock of a 12-gauge
and smashed the old man's face.
Jason arrived then and the boy
begged for it, right here, he shrieked,
pounding his chest, brandishing arms,
by which example your neighbor meant
whoever fails to contrive a tribe,
lights their own bed on fire.
You started reminding yourself not to
stand before windows, bunkered all day
in blue light, drawing the shades at dusk.
I can't read people anymore, you said,
and it seemed clear you'd flouted
the margin of error, mistook tolerances,
as when the District Judge warned
not to try and Jew him down on the sentence.
What to think then of your wanting to
appear diplomatic about a shove from behind
or who to trust when every face in a room
blanked and you could smell the unease
everybody felt about your asking why.
What's the half-life of pretending you're alive,
of being lulled every time the white pines
filled with mourning doves you never saw
arriving ahead of winter storms
and suddenly they were at the window,
perched on limbs, shoulder-to-shoulder,

backs to the wind, at ease, eyes half-closed.
You can almost feel the lull
purring through the glass, the radio bulletin
warning the passes are drifted shut
and the highway closed.

FROM THE END OF WINTER

It's risky to pull him from that place
between bare roots and icy spume.
The volunteer brigade will wait for spring
when the highwater drops to grapple
under debris in the eddy below the mill race.
That's where the drowned lodge in ice,
dressed as when reported missing
in a t-shirt and blue jeans, minus a sneaker
found twenty-five miles downstream.
Since his mother took up residence here
and began her vigil, weeks unspool
false hopes that scald and break like fever.
She's holding out for too much
and for so long, it sours the air
with sick room scent.
She won't permit him to bear
the blame for stumbling drunk and headfirst
over the balustrade into the river.
She ignores the hours elided
from date books, departures delayed,
the rendezvous agreed to but missed,
the entire holiday elapsed before anybody
asked why he failed to arrive.
It's that day again that arrives
every March when people here
lose their nerve and start to dig
behind the garage where neighbors can't
see us shoveling through corn snow
all the way down to the brittle grass,
raking it with our fingers, asking,
Who's there?
Whose little breath is that we hear?

TO THE ANGEL OF FORGETTING

If you passed in the street, you saw
Owl House lit up, heard a woman
shriek and a man wishing
she'd stop. One day after the war–
almost a lifetime ago–she felt
happy, at ease. Eyes clamped shut,
now she batted aside ghosts,
fought back blind in defense
of the lost no one will summon again.
And with all the windows
thrown wide, carrying on like that
late into the night. If you stopped
to listen, even blocks away
you would have felt her grief
the next day. Every room
inside of Owl House hovered
like a moth in a blossoming pear.
They could hardly bear to speak of it
again–that blistering rue,
sour herb of memory.

A BLANK DAY

That gap in August, a vagrancy
in the record you kept,
reverie roving its emptiness,
the cipher for sons to reckon with
why you wrote before and after,
traveled toward and departed from,
and nobody between gathered
bouquets laced with mint
or built a basswood arch
woven with cedar boughs.
A pale spider undisturbed inside
curled umbels of wild carrot,
that day awaits restoration
the way a soul awaits the moon
in a forest you lived a lifetime
at the edge of, distant
as a whip-poor-will
calling from the night of time.

PERIPHERIES

Dead forty years and now this
obverse glimpse of him, the District Judge
saying he met my father–
Marvin, right?–and they shared a cab
from Hopkins Field to Terminal Tower.
This is just the sort of prank
he would play on us–
departing the crumpled fuselage,
the escape artist who passed through
the Alembic we thought
distilled the man to spirit. The stink of it
an illusion, my mother's hysteria.
Instead, he just slipped away
into a life approximate to ours.

::

We were crossing the hills
north of Yakima at dusk in October
and Tahoma cast a conical shadow into the sky–
a diffuse fuchsia impinging upon
a vast absence angling upward
and toward the east.

::

In June, in Andalucía
we stand on a fortress wall,
the wind rising toward us from
cork oaks and orange groves,
the reservoir a vertical kilometer
below, water glittering silver,
a deeper blue welling up,
and there–between

particles of light, blinding to look at—
six falcons hang stationary
in a column of rising air.

::

The original becomes so familiar
we forget to look past the frame,
misperceive the calculus of a hinge
at the edge of a second painted board
that swings wide and reconfigures
the pattern, from the edges of which
we pitch ourselves into another
hoar-frosted alpine meadow,
a sunny morning in mid-winter,
an entirely new spectrum replicating
infinitely under our feet.

::

How else might I imagine
my father's cosmic treachery?
In Cleveland, no less, not Utah,
at the University Library,
where my mother says she saw him
grinning at her
through the stacks in a dream.

AND HURRYING TO CATCH THE 43

I jumped on just as the bus
lumbered from the curb and swung
wide around an old woman,
just lying there in the street,
a crushed finch,
under the grille of a pickup
piled full of plaster slats
and drywall debris, her plaid trolley
flattened, the carton of milk
pooling with blood
under the scarf knotted at her chin.
Old men beneath a ginkgo
overturned their chessboards,
shouted lamentations and pointed
as diplomatic SUVs swerved
onto side streets and sped away.
The young man who ran her over
was squared off with a witness,
but no sirens careered through traffic,
rescue wasn't on its way, and nobody
kneeled to say the words needed
to ease her soul across the threshold
of Kenyon and 17th Streets.

WHISKEY & CRANK

That's an alarming sound,
the hard *plunk* of one cobble
slamming into another in Rock Creek,
the snowmelt at full thrust,
a force like the grunt of people
hurling their bodies at each another–
the spear tackle at midfield
that summons the stretcher
and high-speed collisions on the far curve
that send stock cars spinning
out of control, bleachers full of fans
jumping to their feet with a roar.
Like Rachel, who just told the party
she used to mix whiskey and crank
while Mitch lay helpless on the floor,
wanting it. She thought she hated him,
but felt a bewildering joy
every time she slammed the needle
into his thigh and emptied the syringe.
If pain burned through euphoria
the way a cigarette burns through tissue,
his groans were a sign of
his unwillingness to yield to not being.
They took that erotic risk
and swore to keep each other alive.
In the creek, brimful at our feet,
one cobble pummels another
with the monstrous force of flood
and Mitch takes Rachel's hand in his–
all that water to irrigate alfalfa
on the outwash plains miles below us,
the distances there already turning
green in whatever time remains.

FIRASAH

The window glass balanced at the point
we see through mirrors, she stepped from cedars
tonight, her grandmother hovering
behind me in reflection at the kitchen door,
each of us a different threshold.
The moon and its quarters
have shifted one into another a hundred times
since last she landed here at Owl House,
hauled her little boat up the beach
and trampled the moss to our gate.
If falling for that trick of light was folly,
I meant only to glimpse a wonderment
in some future July in the Wallowas,
when that child's a grown woman,
who I held in my arms
as a newborn, her forebears
ghosting across her face in waves–
that language of souls we choose from
alone. For the migrant alone, may the air
at the edge of a snowbank
someday fill with balm as she kneels
beside her father, as I once did,
the forest just waking up, the sweetness of it
drawn deeply into their lungs.

SIGNAL FIRES

April bounds forth into the meadow
and we rush outside
into the plainspoken light–
look at what lumpen we've become!
We wrestle each other out of our clothes
and egrets flare in willows,
brittle gill lifts its white cap from rotted bales
and out from under a pile of boards, a mouse
flees its nest, a paradise
woven from cedar bark and milkweed silk.
Brimful with intent, cottonwood buds
are turning red, grow sticky
and fill the breeze with balm.
Let allegiance fall toward households,
beginnings we believe in–these goldfinches
making a game of tackling dandelions
and pecking seeds from the air.

THE SPRING CLASSICS

We were leafing through junk store boxes
filled with postcards from *La Belle Époque*
and found among those cozy, hand-tinted pastels
four underexpose black and white snapshots–
a farmstead bombarded by artillery,
a mass grave in a field, the tight ranks
for enlisted men on a slope
below their officers, who lay above them
under larger crosses and behind
pickets someone bothered to whitewash.
There's a coal barge half-submerged
in its haven, a high street lined by rubble
in a village, but no people in sight,
only a few plane trees milling about,
charred by calamity. It had to be
France or Belgium in the spring of 1917.
The following spring young Harry Martinson
worked as a day laborer there,
shoveling bullet casings from the trenches.
Stranger yet, is how, during Lent,
popular bicycle races, the Spring Classics,
pour across those fields–*La Doyenne,*
La Flèche Wallonne, *L'Enfer du Nord*,
that bump along those cobbled,
muddy farm lanes aficionados call *le pavé*.
The countryside's grown up now
in lush pastures and impudent forest,
and everyone's favorite riders in the peloton
move in weird synchrony across the hills.
Full of local ale, fans await the breakaway
and some become so unhinged,
they strip naked and run in the mud
alongside riders, shoving their bikes forward,

shouting *allez! allez!* because they believe
this will embolden their heroes to overcome
the pain and fatigue evident in their faces.

REAL GOOD

It's Wednesday night in the late 1970s
and Kirk Bishop is broadcasting
from Ciro's Lounge live on WVKO,
where, it so happens it's Ladies Night
and in our apartment off Chittenden Ave
we're getting up for the downstroke
before we board the love train
and ride the rollercoaster to
love to love you, baby,
and when the mothership lands,
we change to the midnight train
and Kirk Bishop, make of this
whatever you wish, spins "Dr. Feelgood,"
beseeching the dance floor
to join at the chorus, "Ciro's Ladies–
how's that man make you *feel*?"
A few bars later, the urgencies of their reply
had gone on already far long enough,
were too many and so strong
a whole lifetime couldn't contain it,
that crying out at closing time
for somebody to at least, please, try.

A TOAST ON MIDSUMMER'S EVE

It's more bewildering than sad
how we brought baskets
and found no boletes.
Back in shadows under pines,
snowbanks and granite slabs still
radiate a chill old as December.
Whoever hears earthbound pleas
and no matter how depleted
our future stores, we'll make a picnic
tonight in your name, slice cheese
fragrant as meadow grass,
and share a crust of bread.
We fill our glasses with wine
and the first pour tastes, as it always does,
of cheerfulness and teasing
and by the second we kiss, brimful
with tears for our parents
and childhoods pending appeal.
Fulfilling the third, we laugh,
clink to good health and toast
the young, the guileless and unborn–
a thousand years more aspirations
to dream the limits of.

A TOAST TO HEAVENLY BODIES

The fire brigade paraded past at noon
and when friends introduced them
over the rat-a-tat-tat of drums,
neither heard the other's name,
so now they invent–*Andreas*, she thinks,
the adventurer, and he, *Ingrid*,
most lovely of all. She leans her head
on her sister's shoulder, listening to a joke,
then laughs in noble profile,
her nose, chin, breasts backlit
by the evening sun, pleased to know a man
aches at the very sight of her skin.
The affair going on in their heads now
urges them to forsake data entry,
administrative assistance, the commute
to and from. The new life unfolds
in a Land Rover together in the Andes
driving from Bogota to Fitzroy. Clods of clay,
we too fell into our fates and set this table
for them under a linden tree, here, tonight
in the realm of the already determined
and we're happy, too, they've mistaken
this smorgasbord for falling in love again–
to hearts full of aspirations,
to the divine glow that pours right through you.

BELOW MEDICINE BOW PEAK

Hours ago at the horizon
the full August moon swelled
then climbed the ecliptic toward midnight.
Who could sleep at this altitude?
I wander a maze of granite,
my shadow glittering cold
on a boulder in the meadow.
In a crevice a thousand years of freezing
and thawing opened, I crawl inside.
The surface is hard but smooth as flesh
and incandescent, still warm
from the heat of afternoon.
I press my hands to each
shining surface and ask to close the gap,
let ions sputter awake and stream
through the thin salt and water solution
that is, for reasons of its own,
the electrolyte of love
flowing one to the other.

HOW DO I REMEMBER THEM?

They ran wild, swerving down
township roads north of Alliance, Ohio
tossing empties of Carling Black Label
into borrow pits, ditched their clothes
and swam to an island in the lake,
where they happily fucked away
the late summer nights of 1957.
Their faces aglow under the moon,
marsh lights and lightning bugs
pulsed to a chorus of peepers
and whip-poor-wills—all those buoyant
anthems fulfilled the countryside
with ardor, and I was there with them
afterwards in the front seat
of that gleaming Coup de Ville,
where I remain to this day,
nearing the end of life, their bodies
strong and dark and breathing beside me
as dawn brims a crest of hills.

IN THE LAND OF 1,000 DANCES

We'd forgotten how to feed a child
you sometimes have to keep the beat,
dance a shuffle, dance a waltz,
sing some joyous scat
over mashed peas and pureed squash
or do the Camel Walk and slip
a cheery oat and milk on a spoon
into the little full moon of his mouth,
that is, when doing the Boogaloo
dozy still dotes on Mary's oats
the same as ever. We do the do
and no matter how old we are,
we still carry passports from
the Land of 1,000 Dances,
a photo we show at borders–
oh, baby baby–the one with oatmeal
smeared in our hair, marinara
rouging our ears, a strange slurry
clogging one nostril, bib-trough
full of mango slugs. And floating there
above all that, our happy, abiding
and clownish grin. We do the Watusi,
the Hustle, the Double Bump,
trying our best to distract you
with Major Lance's funky monkey,
hoping you smile and laugh, "Yes!"
Let this *yes* make us all smile and laugh,
"Yes?" Child, please join us as evening
darkens toward the inevitable bath
and soap stinging in your eyes,
because we really have to carry on
like this, twisting the night away
and maybe it's all going to work out

and someone is saving the last dance
for you and me and this dance
is all about the boy with polio
who wrote that song and gave it all
its pathos, that impossible, aspiring
part of ourselves, wobbling toward
the beloved on crutches, who holds us
to her breast and in whose arms
we long to live our lives again.

BLACK WALNUTS

I fell from a great tree. That man
slung burlap sacks full of walnuts over his shoulder,
carried the load into the cellar
and said, "Here, Dragoneer,"

handing off his burden, "We make with the anvil."
He used a ballpeen to crack open the shells
and I scraped the meat into a bowl
with a three-penny nail.

A stranger bought the farm
and cut the trees down. The anvil's all that's left now
from the estate, though I found
a few trees in a fencerow, this one

along Blackhawk Trail,
where I kneel in late October
and rake my fingers through grass
that man dissolved into,

my hands and knees stained by the oily husks.

THE WOE THERE IS IN MARRIAGE

I visited the gravedigger to borrow his spade.
"No problem," he said,
but insisted that he'd dig the hole.
We chose a plot where the crowds thinned out.
The headstones were older out there,
limestone rotted and sigils eaten by moss.
He heaved up a few shovelfuls of brown bones.
Up came a curled spine and ribcage of a child,
and then a real prize, "Lookie here!"—
the palomino I'd forgotten, a gift when I was six,
lifted like a relic from its vault in the earth.
The hole looked big enough and it was all mine.
Later, my wife and I stood side by side,
staring out the picture window on Pleasant Place.
She wept and acted like she couldn't hear me
telling her, "I'm not really dead."
The spectral grids of suburbs had yet
to appear in those fields, where trolly tracks
led off into poverty grass
dusted in starlight. She seemed younger
than when I met her, standing there
alone in the blue light.

TRESPASSES

We were sharing a growler
and Bruce said he'd heard earlier that week
about an old pioneer family that ranches
on tribal allotments, who he guessed
hadn't given any thought to who
their guests might be when they invited
the watershed council to their ranch.
I asked him what he meant by that
and he said they withdrew the offer
when tribal elders RSVP-ed.
I sat and let the reasons for that sink in
and Bruce wondered about the objects
in their house that the ranchers
didn't want the elders to see. Objects,
I told him Agnes Martin said,
are too aggressive. They ran her out of town
you know? Who? Who did they run out?
Agnes Martin, I said, pouring out
two more pints. I like this Double Hazy
Bruce said, holding his glass to the light
and so probably not the time to explain how
she'd got herself crosswise with her dean
during her first term at the Normal School.
He told her to leave and meant leave town
by dark. It was getting darker on the porch
and I told Bruce she lived in the cabin
along Geckler Lane, because he'd remember it–
the red one they burned down
to build an optometrist's office.
Bruce took a schulck and I told him
I thought she must have said that
about objects later, when she turned

her back on turmoil and started seeing
in her mind small grids she scaled up
to a knowable range of light.

ALONG THE TROLL-LØYPA

—two old women joined our train
at a crossroads above Trondsmyra
on New Year's Day, everyone outside
early, making our way together
in long twilight, shouting hellos
across thresholds along the trail,
our ritual of looking always
in two directions at once.
Whenever the old women paused
to strew sacks of breadcrumbs
saved for waxwings, we waited
until they caught up, then skied on
toward Nordseter. At trail's end,
the birds settled as a cloud into willows,
standing by, as the women declared
farvell, adø—their voices granite slabs
struck apart by hammers.
One took off her skis and stood
at the bus stop, waiting for the 14:30.
And tossing her hand, the other
signaled the waxwings,
who lifted as one and followed her
up the trail and all the way back
to Trondsmyra in the fog.

EINFÜHLUNG

I followed midnight
down its path through spruces
to the water's edge.
Skifts of ice
broad as lotus leaves
drifted past on the tide.
Up the hill above the fjord
in the warm honey of her cottage
I mistook the tenor of her
eye-shine and lustrous hair.
Over her shoulder, time
unspooled its oblivions
behind her, in the churchyard
farther up the hill,
where candles guttered
all night over graves.
Among the moss-draped boulders,
I couldn't fathom it.
What solitude do men stray into
at the middle of our lives?
What is it that I can't find
the word for and no way to say it
short of barking at her
tenderness toward being?

SONG OF EXTINCTIONS

Blue-toed skink, speckled cuckoo, borax vetch,

yellow-finned dace, nutcracker pine, wire cress,

Wy'east penstemon, rock grouse, Imnaha wooly elderberry,

sage lettuce, milk lark, horned whitebark frog,

Roth's milkweed, Mary's common blue, Ian's checkerspot whale,

Lahontan swallowtail, Aneroid wolverine, Wallowa blue alder,

Cayuse Lamprey, Kenton vole, Stolen sun peach,

Republican black cherry, love apple, Little Creek meadow foam,

Gillis red squirrel, Bridge of the Gods dolphin, Grande Ronde crow maple,

Sohappy salmon, Sohappy clarkia, Sohappy blue wheatgrass–

MISERERE

Give me back the gladness of Your rescue

After forty years, I emailed B–
who was decent toward me
that one year we were friends,
and I sent him this penitential psalm
in the shape of light in fields
bordered by birch trees.
That year my mother ran off
to salvage whatever life was left
after my father died, her people
took me in, and surely they had to
have known B–'s grandparents,
who like them were young in 1929
and raising their grandchild, too.
A gentleness like theirs was hard
to fathom much less welcome
and they died before my anger
stilled. B– wrote back
that he didn't believe
I recalled that year or him.
But the psalm he recognized
as his orthodox liturgy and listened
through an entire afternoon
of his own late middle age, certain
his image of the two of us alone
in small rooms nations apart,
was the true one and signified,
if anything,
a silence too late to break.

FIRST NIGHT OUT SINCE YOU DIED

The night of the solstice, maybe three hours
passed in darkness before morning
paled the sky in the east.
We were out that night, together again,
visiting friends on the savannah
west of Spokane and after dinner
strayed into the garden our hosts
planted decades ago, the edges grown feral–
rows of lavender and rosemary
entangled, a corner commandeered
by rhubarb and spearmint
vining toward the wellhead.
At midnight, we paused along Deep Creek–
O hospitable world!–
dreaming only of smiles and years to come
of summer nights like that together,
peepers chorusing glories in the alders,
nightjars dodging under the scales of Libra.

TZADIK MOSHE

That morning years ago in Berlin,
as we waited for you to be born,
we already were walking
toward you through the Tiergarten,
in silence and falling snow,
when two red foxes
dashed across the Reichstag lawn.
Ghosts, we thought, of all that was wild,
a world rarely stumbled upon.
It's always closer than we think,
this wonder, not a singular event,
even in the monochromatic snow,
but many tremors, a braid
of souls rippling through us.
It took months to find our way
to that hushed flat in another city
the 18th century erected and war
burned to ash.
Your mother heard us knocking
and lifted you into our arms
at the threshold. We didn't so much
hold you as you beheld us in the gravity
of your gaze, that summons wanderers
from the wilderness
to the nakedness of the word.

THE READINESS IS ALL

Hours and miles later
in the mountains, an unbroken
ring of lupine blues sipping
from the black mirror of a puddle
below a seep, a bog orchid
gleaming in its glade nearby,
and one song sparrow's voice
floating on azure noise of the creek
swollen with snowmelt.

::

This morning on a siding
in the marsh, camouflaged by dry tules,
a military train a hundred flatcars long
idled, loaded with armored dozers,
bridgers, mine rollers and breachers
that combat engineers follow on maneuvers.

::

Sunlight's so aggressive at this altitude
it blisters the young,
though these weeks since the solstice,
we've watched the shadow
the older maple casts along the devil's strip,
shift northeastward and now
in the harshest afternoon sun
it shades the younger trees.

HILLEL'S PARABLE OF BURDENS

At the High Holidays long ago,
an old couple traveled on foot
between valleys separated by mountains,
leading their donkey by a frayed rope,
Bobo, who bore baskets of dry figs
and dates they'd trade for oil and wheat.
Three nights from home,
they pitch their tent in a cedar grove
and the rug floor trapped hornets
inside a malice-filled, mucus-sealed nest.
The ground rippled–
all that madness going on just below
the moon-lit faces of those two sleepers,
while Bobo kneeled in the meadow.
The night cooled, the nest stilled and
in the morning, the couple stretched–
never slept better in all our lives!–
and broke camp before the sun
warmed and hornets emerged ready
to beset the next passersby.
Outside a village, the couple paused
to pick blackberries, and later,
the woman's ankles swelled, so they stopped
as she soaked in a creek whose water
ran cold over her feet. A small frog
swam up out of the deep, climbed her shin
and each dwelled an hour in the other's calm.
The light air stirred the aspens–
a drier, thinner register of sound,
a tinkling almost drowned out
by the monotony of the creek
and its jade dream. Bobo brayed at them
to mind the daylight and waited

for the old man to tighten the sheepshank
his grandfather taught him to tie
when he was a boy. Happy to journey's end,
the couple returned to their garden,
crickets singing at the gate. Bobo
wandered across the paddock to his shed
and–

Shammai, have we failed
our duty to The Law, if we remember
the old couple's laughter beside the jade pool
or Bobo's minding the hour
and burden he still bore?

Jerusalem of Grass

ALLEGIANCES

East across the cut hayfields,
Arabian mares were corralled
behind hawthorn and nailed boards.
When day dawned clear,
steam rose off their backs
and burr-tangled manes,
the air around them sweet
with the odor of damp burlap.
Each seemed patient, standing
still where I saw them last
at dusk the day before.
At what hour in the dark
did they kneel
and fall asleep in snow
or just before daybreak
jackknife onto their legs again?

The woman who chose me
groaned awake in the loft,
her weight shifting
on the plank floor above.
Cedar shakes ignited
and popped in the stove.
A ray of sun
lowered through the canyon
below Olson Peak
and I looked for the colt
who stood among the mares,
their allegiances steadfast.

My life had answered almost to nothing.
Every afternoon that winter, I saw families
riding freights west to Seattle,

and one night a man wandered
from the railyards with family in tow.
He asked for directions
to the Poverello House,
where I knew they'd be turned away,
the dorms full every night,
the meals already eaten.

I heard so many garbled voices–
my own, the shouting braves
in parking lots, the President
and his parochial connivers,
the whole exhausted horde of us
giddy with betrays,
laughing at the folly of love.
Waking, my hands worried
the swelling belly of my bride,
another pulse drumming deep
in her syncopated blood,
a single irritating grain
spun into a living pearl.

And one morning as I sat
at the window looking out at the fields
before dawn, a yellow spider
with eyes like a string of emeralds
dropped from the ceiling
onto my wrist and I heard my love say
to hurry, look quick–the horses
had broken from their corral
and bolted through the snow,
stopping only at the crest of the field
to wait for the colt to cross
before they descended together with the sun
into the hoar-cover canyon below.

BAINBRIDGE DAIRY

On a rare day of sun,
we followed her path across fields,

the clear way she'd found
from one pasture to the next,

her habit of passing through
deep sod and hollows

where blackberries canes swelled
and strained toward light.

Clouds lifted from the Sound
and far off across the water

the Olympics
lunged from the sea like whales.

With the laughter of gulls
we passed through scotch broom,

under maples into old fields
where her mind still sweats

in the leaf-fall of her orchard,
in the scum of rotted fruit,

and we came there as lovers
one afternoon in November,

trespassing on a rare day of sun
when nobody saw us

or bothered to tell us to leave.

A FRIEND PHONES FROM NEW YORK CITY

telling me that the streets there
remind her of Calcutta.
A thin laughter fills
twenty-five hundred miles of wire,
sagging in gentle arcs
across the winter prairie
and I think about tomorrow,
how I'll get off the grave at 7 a.m.
and start across town
in the small dawn of January.

At the Husky station,
I'll stop for gas and a man
will step between pumps
staring a 10-cent coffee
steady in his hand.
He'll pass under the sodium lights
and vanish into river fog.

I see him every morning,
sitting out of the snow
on the backstairs
of the Western Montana Clinic,
constructing his day, the various
gestures at routine
that empty the hours of cold
between meals and sleep.

Under the Dog Days sun
he might have joined
the beautiful swains lounging
in the shade of the County Welfare,
hustling his nuts and joking

with shabby girls who shriek
a loneliness so long
America will never end.

My nights off I wake
to the banging window
in the cabin loft, gnashing my teeth,
jaws gripped on the lost
faces glimpsed in a dream
like peripheral lights
flashing past at street corners.

A friend phones from NYC,
a place as unreal to me as Calcutta
and all I can think of, hearing her
detached laughter through the receiver,
is how, tomorrow, as the sun
waxes pale in the Hellgate,
streets will fill with cars
pressing forward, obedient, diurnal,
and in ever doorway
there will be laughter
arriving as if from far away inside.

IN TONGUES

Three months without rain
since the Kalispell archer
"legally harvested" an albino bear,
grainfields on the plains
are a checkerboard of char,
trout in dry riverbeds rot,
the greens I bring in from the garden
sour like clay on my tongue.

In the published photo, the bear
lolls across the archer's knees–
a two-year-old sow, gutted,
forelegs bound with wire,
on display in a barroom
crowded with trophies and men.

Pink flesh, yellow-white hair,
sickle moons under claws
the color of human fingernails,
hers is the skin men want
to crawl inside of
and begin mutilating themselves.

This morning at dawn, flames
exalted on Diamond Mountain,
the well sputtered sulfur gas from the tap,
ashes rained on the shake roof,
smoke darkened the sun
to a cinnabar sphere at noon.

After days of fevers, my sons
laughed in their sleep,
jabbering gaily with nobody

in tongues that summoned
a squall from the canyon.
Rain rapped a moment at the window.
No promise, nothing sinister,
just a few damp welts raised in dust.

All summer, I've tried to trace
coincidences like lines of grain
swirling in polished mahogany,
but now all events diverge
from the smashed atoms our lives become
and though we still trade in futures,
a year without harvest will come.

KADDISH

After the gas tanks break
and wings fold back like swallows,
after the rain and flames, father,
lead me back to the ark
of uncluttered light,
the veins of your wounded throat.

Let me pray at last
in acres of alsike and rye
on this hillside north of Massillon,
where the Tuscarawas rises
and leeches wait at shore for us
to slough our broken skins,
bob downstream with the swift
current and sludge.

Give me to the green Jerusalem of grass,
where you sailed from the ignited sky
above quailing maples.
Lead me back
from the river's greasy shore,
press my hands to your punctured throat,
show me smuts and molds
where they grow
in the split hollows of your wrists and ribs.

Give me to the green shoots
that hold us fast
to this thick, downward
whirling earth, the healed fault
where you fell,
the acres of uneroded grass.

ACROSS THE GREAT DIVIDE

for Hollis & Laura Summers

We stayed indoors all morning
while a steady wet snow fell
and concealed distant fields.
My sons played in their room,
tossed cheap toys and shrieked
with glee at every crashing noise,
while I straightened the kitchen,
put dishes in cupboards,
swept and mopped the linoleum
and went to my desk to dust
and rearrange the river rocks
that glowed in blue snow-light
at the fogged windowsill.
I touched each rock to my face—
pure, indivisible facts, smooth
and cool for millions of years.

Yesterday, we visited my teacher
in his living room, where he lies
on a cot near his own window
and oak tree—Hollis and oak
both sick with years, lopped
and drugged.
                        I read him Yeats,
"Proud, open-eyed and laughing"
and he swam up from the dark,
opened his eye and laughed,
"Raspberries—I despise them!"
A cardinal landed and pecked
at suet Laura hung on a feeder
in the oak Hollis said was his

tragic, half-starved twin, a sapling
the year Lincoln was born.
Later, as we drove home
10,000 blackbirds
streamed up ahead of us
from the salt-covered road.

All my household set to order,
I stood at the window this morning
watching oak trees stagger off
into the heavy snow and heard
a singer's voice from the radio,
a woman singing so calm and fierce,
I held still and stopped breathing,
"and I find myself on a mountainside,
where the rivers change direction,
across the Great Divide."
My infant son fell hard in the other room,
a loud thump on the floor, a stunned
gasp, a lusty scream—how lucky
to be called to urgent facts
surging toward us, cold and sober
as river stones.
                    Down the hallway,
ducking through doorways
in our dingy little house
and its domestic distractions, I hurried
already holding him in my arms.

REGARDING A NUDE ON DIAMOND MOUNTAIN

I drove below this mountain one morning
five years ago, returning to the cabin
to collect tarps and axes I left
when we moved, too poor to stay
where we first lived together
far from towns and people.
In the anonymous twilight,
snow lowered into the valley,
a blue tide climbed over the dark
evergreen slopes of Mineral Ridge.
Children shrieked,
bolted in and out of yellow barn lights,
their faces thrown open
daring the dwindling night.
I drove by unrecognized, an intruder
passing along the road into pines,
recalling my way there, almost
lost in the accumulating snow.

::

She steps from her clothes
and stands on the bluffs
naked high above the Blackfoot
at Johnsrud Bend.
Loosened from its braid,
her hair fans across her shoulders
and reaches clear
down the curve of her spine
to full hips and thighs.
She stretches onto a weightless
tiptoe, turns into the wind,
her hair lifting behind her,

an auburn banner
unfolding a mile above the valley
and hayfields raked into windrows.

::

And like a bear waking
from his dream of stumps and grubs,
who lifts his stinging face
from a creek that braids
across the slovenly world each spring,
I shiver, cut free from
the underworld where I slept off
my grief, free maybe as she is
rising from the dust beside me
on the sixth great day.
Shedding denim, pine needles and dust,
my legs brittle dry sticks,
I leave my refuge in the pines,
welcome in our home
and wobble toward her on bare feet,
in my own body again.

The Kingdom at Hand

//

THE KINGDOM AT HAND

> *but where is what I started for so long ago,*
> *and why is it yet unfound?*
>
> —Walt Whitman, "Facing West from California's Shores"

1.

An older man wants to know if my generation
hasn't given up the Romantic spirit of his youth
and chosen instead to embrace decadence?
But he doesn't really blame us for that,
"What kind of world did we leave for you?"
And again before I can answer, he wants to know,
"Do you have children? What do you tell them
the world was like when you were still young?"

He expects me to join in and gripe, as though
I'd tell my children something glib like
Give up! Your planet is dying. As though
maybe I'd keep them up at night listening
to weeping that travels from city to city
along high voltage lines that hiss
in humid air, leaking kilowatts of defeat.

And even if everything is weeping—
fields of corn, quarried granite, books
that absolutely refuse to look us in the face,
refrigerators weeping into narrow drains,
dentures that do and don't fit, thrushes,
maples, priceless grain rotting in fields,
or haircuts, heaps of junk tires, defiant
people peering at us from underpasses,
even millionaires with excellent hygiene—
all as good as dead, all weeping.

It's merely apocalyptic sorrow, so much waste,
le fin de siecle, the millennial nightmare.
It's the sense of something big coming our way
after years without rain, wind worrying the pines,
driving ahead of it the scent of fires,
flocks of panicked birds, and by evening,
the ocean, the reek of salt, fish, and storm.

Something is ending now, but it's more than
the 20th century or Soviet Union, more than theory,
justice or law—those dying old men
whose hands flutter like moths at windowsills.
And it's far more than you or me at five a.m.,
opening boxes of old LPs, discovering the *Eroica*
has vanished, Beethoven's scratchy music
gone out of the black, spiraling grooves.

And what remains? Only a puffed-up
Romantic portrait of Napoleon, unhorsed,
a frightened little emperor, retreating from
the ferocious sound of a composer's will.

It's all gone wrong and gone wrong again!
Bankers and corporate lawyers occupy the Commune.

The day opens and closes and opens
its 10,000 eyes, the marble sky
dropping heaps of gold in weeds at my feet—
gold like long hair tossed down from the Tower,
though what resides up there is bitter
and the Host turns our tongues to char.

So what do I tell my young sons about
the glorious past, the infinite landscape
of possibilities just around the corner?
Should I tell them there's no such thing

as gravity, no drag chains, no weight,
no limitations to desire? Or should I
show them how evil is streamlined, precise,
pure, and above all, profitable, source
of every comfort but satisfaction?

Or show them a woman (it could be a man)
standing alone at the verge of vast,
treeless high desert, thirteen decades
after the last pioneers died and took
their impossible longing underground.
Why is she weeping? Earth curves away,
willing to let her go, and yet
that woman (she's from D.C.)
quails from the edge where flat shadows
sweep across rabbitbrush, greasewood, and sage.

Shadows? Perhaps,
but what else could they be? Clouds?
Mountains? Great birds? You? Me?

2.

It's taken three days of wandering
a little hungry, dirty, and tired,
but now I'm walking with enough affection
to at least suspect the sadness present
here in this deep basin glaciers gouged,
this creature as alive and dying as I am.

Standing on a ridge above the Grande Ronde,
it's clear what the river remembers.
In wheatfields that were tule marshes
or abandoned meanders before this valley
was trenched, drained, and diked, long before

this valley was plowed and sown to wheat
by high-minded pioneer farmers—months now
after spring floods have receded, those fields
are shallow lakes again, as they should be,
and each rubbish-filled abandoned meander
forms a sinuous emerald line of grass.

This year, the wheat crop will fail.
But the river's genius is no less present
than a century ago, when history migrated here
from Ohio, Missouri, and Illinois—that green
and thriving prairie, land of long, humid
summers, as painfully rich as its soil was deep.

What did the Oregon pioneers think,
having crossed weeks of gray desert,
to crest this ridge high above the valley
and see below them 50,000 acres
of impassable marsh! Even knowing that
their Promised Land lay only across another
two mountain ranges and high desert plateau,
after so many months and thousand miles,
they must have suspected a fraud.

What longing rose up in them? In spite
of their disastrous intentions—draining marshes,
burning away willow thickets and galleries
full of cottonwood—no native part of Europe,
much less their Midwest, flourishes here,
no trails wind through canopies of sumac,
no wild cherry or hickory, no beechnut,
white oak or sycamore, no loud thrum of bees
working white clover, no snapping turtle
the size of a Sunday platter asleep
one morning on a warm doorstone.
One pioneer woman, who began her journey

west from Iowa, writing in her journal,
"Hurrah, boys! All ready! Gee up
Tip and Tyler and away west we go!"
four months later spent a sleepless night
in this valley at a hot sulfur spring
ringed by sun-bleached antlers. Her cows
were dying and her child lay sick with fever.
"I felt as if I were in a bad place, and was glad
when morning came and we left."

That's the terror of vastness, of a country
refusing to be what we desired, a loneliness
that drove that woman sleepless and sick
toward a familiar, if only promised,
lush green valley—free for the taking!—
just one mountain range east of the Pacific.

4.

In June sunlight below snowbanks
at 7,000 feet, we rested an hour
under Hurwall Divide, and I recited my sons
a poem by Bai Juyi. Later that evening,
over dessert bowls of canned peaches,
a retired Red Army officer, a survivor
of the Long March, exile in the caves of Yenan,
and later, prison, torture, and re-education,
laughed, "Bai Juyi! I would have guessed.
Americans read only sullen bureaucrats!"
He threw back his shoulders and recited
Percy Shelley in a thick northern accent,
"Wild Spirit, which art moving everywhere;
Destroyer and preserver, hear, oh hear!"

And our talk veered from politics to poetry,
turned aside from any words for students
littering Tiananmen Square, swerved hard
toward its metaphor—Heaven's Peaceful Gate.
Thus we must define first principles,
thesis and antithesis, two yowling mongrels
tied together by their tails, whipped
and eager to continue the old quarrel.
But what metaphor misnames, remains distinct,
distant, it never reaches as far as my table
after dinner, grains of rice and slivers
of wild mushroom sticking to my forearm.
This is the charm (it's no charm at all)
of well-fed, idle thoughts—insular tedium
of evenings in well-tricked homes in the West.

All this vastness of motion, from atom
to mineral to root, river, wind and golden
eagles, all that's given its body by molecules
of air diffusing into space, and I can find
no handhold here more secure than this moment
or the next that words refuse to order.
Paralyzed seven years before he died,
what did Bai Juyi care about our impossible
longing for stasis? "During the day, my feet
are palsied, tottering; in the night, my steps
go striding over the foothills and valleys.
As day and night divide into equal parts,
between the two I regain as much as I lose."

Eight thousand miles across the Pacific
from Heaven's Peaceful Gate, while students
gaped, amazed at the meaning of their blood
that day in June, the father tried to explain
this to his sons who sat, drunk with laughter,
squirming on a boulder, "This mountain divide

is partly the result of orogeny. Say that word,
o-rog-en-y—massive batholiths uplifted by
the simultaneous subduction and overthrust
of colliding continental and oceanic plates.
The older rock crosscut by the younger
volcanic intrusions, those thin, vivid
black and white granitic veins swirling
in grey rock. And those cliffs above us?
The surface pattern will remind you of dry,
cracked mudflats, which is what they are.
Before mountains erupted, this was ocean shore,
and though it's turned on edge now, somehow
it's still fluid, you see, though what you see
appears static, even eternal, always product,
but seldom the inexorable processes."

The solstice sunlight still filled the sky
above Hurwall Divide, and yet I was as far
from my sons' knowing as deer from people.
And the next day, too, I couldn't climb
higher, nor sing madly on any mountainside.
I could say I felt, but could no longer feel,
the play of heat and chill air rinsing
through ice caves alongside the trail—
blue crystals buried deep within rockslides.

But even rubble that preserves fossil water
as a blue, radiant gem, or even the image
of avalanche, is nothing more than a valence,
a willingness of things to cohere or seem to,
a kind of permission to draw near to what
remains always dangerous, unstable.

So it's not the world we've lost we lament,
but the present one from which we remain
distant and distinct. But that old man

who wants to know if I tell my sons the world
was a beautiful place once, laughs at this,
like the retired Chinese officer at dinner
condescending to Bai Juyi. If there is no
uninhabited continent nor undiscovered
archipelago for us to claim like Grim
sailing into Borgarfjord to parcel out Iceland
to kinsmen, then the old man concludes
that suicide (not his, of course) seems like
the sole logic to remedy a ruined world.

5.

One autumn, I traced this glacier-vein,
ascended through rocks blotched with lichens
to the headwaters on the ridge, a dirty,
dwindling ice-field gripping a small cirque.

For months, fools kept making public threats,
lovers of tritium, daring to demonstrate
their obdurate wills, to command the ignition
of entire continents, the abortion of spring.

The sky was awful so close, I gaped upward
at its beginning, nine geese crossing the sun
so close above me, for the first time I heard
air filtering through wings as they hurried
ahead of a storm, invisible still in the north.

But I insisted, there was nothing to flee,
nothing to resist, and it didn't matter to die,
I could let my body crumble there, a puny
measure of carbon, as though it were that simple,
an honest act accomplished in an instant,
a grim, cosmic gesture, it would cost me nothing.

Sunlight drove back every boundary of sky,
five mountain ranges curved toward horizons
and reflected light back across the world, flawless
gold across miles of granite and ice.
But for all I cared, the mountains might
have done me a favor, slammed together,
a cataclysm preempting every folly
I or anyone else might make of life.

But now, in April, in ice-scoured boulders
scattered in the river, where only weeks ago
ice floes piled and groaned sadly, two extinct
silver-green shadows slash past me upstream

where they may spawn in gravel, two of the lives
Adam gave names to, strayed where they least belong–
this spring I was certain would never come,
greeting me freely down by the riverside.

6.

Persistent southwesterly winds shove dunes
slowly across the valley toward foothills,
drifts swallowing whole crowns of cottonwoods
whose bare limb-tips rise from sand, the bark
peeling like beds of snakes shedding skins.

Windward, dunes slope gently toward their ridge,
where the sharp leeward fall forms a crescent
like a horned winter moon in the east at dawn.

Their ridges are long, continuous wave-fronts
of bright sand contrasted against turquoise sky.
In that line flows a grander and elusive image
of ourselves, who, waking in the dark house,

grope forward carefully, until the room
we stumble in arranges itself in our minds
and we move again with confidence and grace.

Winds build off the plateau to the south
and gust with heat. Small sprouts of seeds
tendril open in the damp morning light,
wither at noon, brittle as thin, burnt wire.
Dig down. The sand is moist and dense.
But surface layers are windblown–
a fine salt and pepper mix of rhyolite
quartz and basalt that devils-up and swirls,
a weightless fog or spirit, stinging my skin
and instantly erasing my trail across sand.

That visible surface motion of dunes
is like seeing small flocks of mergansers
fly up at dusk just as the tide turns out,
when the moon lurks low in the spruces
and a ragged sky streams in from the coast.

Digging clams with a friend last spring, a heron
hidden in razor grass croaked, announcing us
as we stepped from shadow onto a moonlit
spit of sand that divided salt marsh from sea.

Wings slapped brackish water, but at first
I couldn't name what I saw, and stared
at a flat ground fog of silver sparks gliding
quietly over the spit and veering off
suddenly to follow the retreating tide.

It was a vision from the Sagas of weird
creatures passing so close to where we dug,
a rare, inexplicable terror in me startled
awake and longed to graze swiftly over water,

over mudflats and moonlit tidepools, spurning
the shore, utterly transformed, free of what I am.

Then I recognized what I saw and relaxed.
It was a flock of red-breasted mergansers,
living things I could name by the flickering
white splotches of their inner wings.

At the far end of the spit, where we stopped
to turn back, a pair of rusty rails led
from mud to dry dock. Up on its blocking
and faintly phosphorescent, a sailboat rotted,
gunwales blotched by glowing lichens and mold.

What is alive with interior light near the sea,
is alive in the dunes, too, patches of soil,
cryptograms that look like nothing more
than gray ashes spread over cracked clay.

It rises from earth a perpendicular inch,
as if a herd of improbably small antelope
stampeded, or like rain-pitted sand, moisture
from a puddle wicked into crystals of frost.

And it's hundreds of years old,
alive as any ancient creature who's left alone.
And like its cousins, those patches of lichen
that blotch alpine boulders, it transforms
inert minerals, excretes fertile soil, husbands
the desert toward a richer world, resists
erosion of flashfloods, stores the run-off,
converts the inorganic into energy.

Without the patient labor of parasites,
nothing would survive. Earth would look
like Mars—lifeless god who lures fools

into his vast landscape of stony ciphers.

Cryptograms flourish wherever anything is
even meagerly alive to feed upon—duff,
cones, aromatic berries and nuts that collect
in gray, dry rings under piñon and juniper.
Or it will cluster in colonies that circle
rabbitbrush, greasewood, and sage. It thrives
even under cactus that cast hardly any shade!

And yet, it's so delicate, once disturbed,
centuries might pass before it heals the wound
of our heavy, mindless haste. When I look up,
trails zigzag scars into dunes, pursuing
something obscure as a moment's desire
that outlives us seven times seven generations.

Strict Linnaeus grouped it in the same class
as mushrooms, coastal ferns, seaweed, algae,
molds, and lichens that grow on rotted wood.
CRYPTOGAMIA, truest metaphor of this poem,
from Greek: *kryptos*, "hidden," and *gamia*, "marriage."

So it's love, flourishing here at my feet
in each dry patch of soil—the first, most joyous
symbiotics! All these lovers casting spores
into the wind, higher, more diffuse than any
pulse of hot sperm, an invisible lovemaking
that carries them aloft 10,000 feet,
and here, too, earthbound, all around us,
belly-to-belly and tongue-to-tongue, secretly
inside us, all this intricate touching of cells,
growing, growing, growing in our lungs!

7.

Sitting cross-legged in red volcanic ash,
my son, who just learned to read and write,
bends over his first journal, note-taking, waiting
for me to climb the switchbacks to him.

In his bright green sweater he is like one
of those young ponderosa pines that fall
as seeds from the canyon rim, where forested
high desert plateau crowds the abrupt edge.
Seeds fall like an amber, whirling rain,
land on narrow ledges, and after thunderstorms,
sprout in an inch of duff and dust, the pale
tap root tendriling into damp granite.

Reaching him, I ask to hear what he wrote.
Each sentence is in future tense! Beginning,
"Tomorrow we will," and ending, "It will be fun!"

I explain the present tense, but he rolls his eyes.
It's too plain-spoken and bland! And it's no use
talking about how longing slanders our lives
and makes us poor. This meal we eat today
never satisfies so much as the promised feast.

Two years ago, illiterate, he would sit
bent over drawings he'd name only after
they were complete: "Beewa Soars Witchery,"
or "What Swallows See at Night." He'd scribble
madly all over a sheet of paper, then recite:
"Lightning cuts through the air, the Immoral
Sword of Baladorn! Claps of air from deep
dungeons of thunder! And the Windy Queen came,
matting down cornstalks with her flying cape,
and squash crawled leafy through the straw!"

Why the caution now before the claim,
a pause of doubt that blurs instinct?
What did they teach him in school that he might
spend his entire lifetime trying to unlearn,
the way every man who limps, after years
of slogging behind, for an hour forgets
his old shame, and suddenly abandoned,
traipses with child-like shrieks of grace?

In the hallways at his school, which smells
of sour milk and paste, hang rows of identical
cotton ball clouds. And there are mosaics
of George Washington, "Father of Our Country,"
and "President of Our Dollar," spelled out
in very pink kidney beans. His eyes are black
turtle beans. He smiles (inasmuch as a slave owner
with wooden teeth ever smiled) a mouthful
of northern navy beans. His ears? Giant limas!

Thumbtacked on the wall opposite one room
are twenty-three leafless trees, each brown
trunk standing isolated in a smudge of watery
blue and green, and in the upper left hand
corner, a small, amorphous slice of a once
golden orb casts its dimmer light to earth.

Chronicles of the Withering State

A MINOR CONTEMPORARY (ON THE EDITOR OF THE CHRONICLES*)*

To contextualize his efforts, curators included this pastel sketch by one of the man's mistresses, depicting an intimacy and animal warmth he failed in every case to bring forth. The same failure presents itself in our own lives: how best to bring forth our mortal forms? Her full breasts, thick hips, the fall of long hair across the clavicle that must have just shuddered like a wing. Or her lover, who is nothing but a thin line uncoiling beside her, stretching toward the border of their bed's heat. In this we recognize that we are, as we fear, a near-emptiness. Our bodies brief radiancies only darkness defines the edges of.

THE CONSOLATIONS OF REVEREND MALTHUS

The same spectacle every autumn: flies swarming at the warm windowpanes. One by one they starve, lose their grip, spiral to the sill, buzz and grow still. In this we acknowledge the approach of winter, famine, pre-destination. Events that reveal elemental law. Our error, however, is our faith in consolation. We insist fate may be located in examples of blind and ordinary persistence, but only because we believe we are exempt from similar misperceptions. We assume that we will close this gap that perplexed the flies and fall through the glass barrier that separates us from kinder gods, those who remain invisible and more restrained than any others we know.

NOVEMBER 1989

What a merry spectacle: patriot anthems, raised fists, a child with a chisel, a plaza thick with a million singers, toppled statuary, tyrants in retreat. But what longed-for triumph will we celebrate next year? Or the years after that? What did we think would become of all our cherished fears, the little horrors we keep like exotic green feathers in a pouch under our ribs? The tangle of assassinations, race riots, wars of attrition, the orange robes of flame, coils of concertina wire, miles of neurotic cinder block, the severed mind, a faulted earth, techniques of crouch and cover–it was part of some miraculous purpose after all! When I was my children's age, the year between the Bay of Pigs and "Love Me Do," I woke one morning after a party, and walked through the house amazed: the furniture overturned, the carpets covered in beer bottles and ashes, a man I didn't know in his briefs passed out in the hallway. Vomit floated in the toilet. On the living room wall someone had sketched Walt Whitman's kind face with a cube of charcoal, and these words spray-painted in a red halo: "If need be a thousand shall sternly immolate themselves for one."

FROM THE ANTHOLOGY OF THE LAST REPUBLIC (I)

Between us and boundless sky
our Maker applies His skills:
red-shifting quasars bruised into being,
clouds of cobalt and magenta gas,
stars coalescing from a bituminous void,
planets and moons like pearls of oil
smeared in a puddle, where we appear:
vague objects scumbled into being.

Our basket of hardboiled eggs and bottles of beer
failed again to bribe the border guards,
and so, we are returning now
in the dark before day, driving
along the pot-holed road through the foothills,
pausing at a roadside shrine
to ask the Virgin of Dry Falls to forgive
the monotony of our sins.

Hope dissolved from our language
as slowly as rock salt dropped in a well
whose water is cold and black
as the skin of plums ripening in August.
Not sweet, not tart.
Rather, something always in between.
Our metaphor: above us incomparable space,
below us a factory working half-shifts,
its stacks glittering, upwind of the city,
our valley draped in clouds of phosphorus.

The fate we are assigned.

FROM THE ANTHOLOGY OF THE LAST REPUBLIC (II) (A FRAGMENT)

Forced to project our lives elsewhere,
we witness an all-entangling sublime
as children led hand-in-hand
under the Capitol dome
on the anniversary of the Senators
being stood against a wall by militiamen.

Later, with our teacher, we gathered
baskets of wild onions and mushrooms
in the forest, filled glass jars
with water from the spring where the Virgin,
raped by our enemies, bled to death, purifying us.
An inconsolable Beauty, this freedom,

impenetrable to us now as old-fashioned script
carved into stones. Our deaths came to signify
our lives, glimpses of what we were–
brief, but unbearable to look at . . .

OF ATTACK

Delirious as wrens, children dance in gravel at recess, their voices muted by gusts of wind. A woman sits alone at the kitchen table, writes, "Geraniums on the windowsill sway toward sunlit glass," then closes her journal and glances at the wall clock. 10:35 a.m. You pause, too, on a county road to watch flocks of white birds descend to the marsh. Are they snow geese or swans? And you don't know which it is you're aware of next, because either way it's already too late: over your shoulder, four bright cylinders arcing beautifully westward across the mountains or that sound, miles distant, the metal larynx of a siren bursting into its deconstruction of melody, a pure, infantile wail of fear.

FROM THE ANTHOLOGY OF THE LAST REPUBLIC (III) (A FRAGMENT)

How hard how hard how hard we prayed
for the distant nest the mind makes,
a warm, woven solitude in which
our mothers felt free to sing to us
in the seamless night, seamless day,
the brilliant eighth notes of April . . .

ROMANTIC ODE

A sorrowful sentimentalist raises his glass: "It will always be October 1962, the handsome young president's face flickering gray at the far end of the cellar. My father had died in the spring and we buried him under a scabby sycamore in Ohio. And now, Kronos stands in breakers just off our shore, a black, menacing cylinder that blocks out the sun, its machinery humming with the inexorable evil of its economic theory. It's cold and mildewy in this cramped room. Sirens and klieg lights sweep across the window and tunnel the perpetual overcast, above which our enemies float, invulnerable as gods."

A PEDAGOGIC PARABLE

As she left the classroom ahead of me, a volume of Chaucer in her arms, Megumi turned and said she had not sat *zazen* in two weeks: "This is why I am so petulant in class!" A moment later, in the lavatory I tried to splash water on my face, but I had no face, in fact, I had no head at all. The excess skin of my neck was tucked neatly into a hole at the middle of my shoulders, clean as an infant's bellybutton after the stub of the knotted umbilicus rots away. I felt compelled by this odd circumstance to quiz my next class on the possibility of living without irony or guile. But they were freshmen and only stared at me in silence. Later, I tried again, with seniors, pointing to a passage from *The Chronicles of the Withering State* about how we await the onset of the Extreme Event, a purifying crisis. During which everyone will lose his head, wanting to avenge himself. Of course, we will brutalize our neighbors. And of course, wells will be piled full of corpses that come out gray and bloated months after. And after the years-long standoff, of course everyone will feel ashamed, repentant and not eager to ever do it again. "No, no, no! Abandon plumb and square!" By which the chronicler meant to advise us that it is always preferable to nail the mezuzah askew at the threshold, remembering to press a kiss to it with your fingers as you enter or leave. To recognize how an African weaver deliberately perplexes the perfected pattern of his design with a bright, errant thread. Or how the ceiling in the abandoned mosque (despite the Arabic precision about the geometries of heaven) draws one's attention upward in awe of its stylized chaos, that humbling, beautiful cartoon of the mind of God. Perhaps even Megumi's odd inflection of a medieval English meter. If not these imperfect forms, headless as we are, to what else shall we bow?

WHATEVER HAPPENED TO OUR OLD REVOLUTION?

A century ago, Walt Whitman, our countryman, our loyal friend, stiff and doddering from strokes, rode a train one morning west out of Denver through the mouth of Platte Canyon and steamed upward for miles to aspen groves at Kenosha Pass, where he spent an hour declaiming, "these vast and formless arrays for reasons of their own," so ecstatic at the sheer immensity of the continent, he almost forgot his train east to Camden to die.

CROOKED LIGHT (ON ARCHEOLOGICAL DISCOVERIES FROM THE LAST REPUBLIC)

I found a fragment of deer skull tangled in weeds at my feet, the crown between antlers where sutures meet, the confluence of great rivers meandering close to the brain. And as with all skulls–of a field mouse or plover, of a porcupine or my own, lying moss-covered beside a creek or bleached white by sun or this one, its eye sockets threaded by bunchgrass and bull thistle–these sutures are the last to come loose, reluctant to release the fertile, knotted density they held inside. Sutures curve and curve again, knitting together the pliant plates of the skull the way lovers touch intricately, as grass welcomes rain after drought. Just a blush of pink remains here along the convoluted seams, the last glint of sun on the rippling current, afterglow of nerve-ends firing, impulses leaping the gap, of crooked, uncontainable light, a smoldering archaic phosphorescence that is still seeping out like water from limestone. Even in mud of mass graves the year after a civil war ends, you see the deliberate volunteers tenderly cradling these inextinguishable lamps.

The Cartographer's Melancholy

//

TILED MOSAIC

At the city gate,
in the damp shadow of limestone
quarried first by slaves and later
by zealots, he knelt. Holy site piled upon

wreckage of holy site, a vertical profile
of conquests. In this way, he found the *Judería*
below the ruins of the Roman bridge–its vandalized
streets and baths full of leaves and broken glass.

::

After making love, he asked to photograph her
staring straight into the lens, where the mirror deflected
the gaze of his squinted eye. A prank they'd play
on whomever might later remark about

that strange expression on her face.
She felt ill-at-ease in that city,
intimidated by threats painted on walls.
She wondered, *Should anything so frank be framed?*

::

Bowing in the urine stench of shadows below wrought iron,
he uncovered the six-pointed star of his namesake–
bright chips of glass inlaid in paving stones. An empty street,
no less claustrophobic now

than during the interregnum, before anarchy erupted
like a virus in the blood. This star. This vertigo
of infinitely repeating patterns
designed to trick the eye.

::

Not the scent of horse, but of Christians.
The tripartite reconstruction of La Sinagoga de Santa Maria la Blanca–
an absurd name, for what was, briefly, a military stable
and now is empty except of light.

And this oddity–the Moroccan who followed the couple
into the sanctuary, half-hidden
behind columns near the door, who raises his hands
to cover his face as he prays.

::

Men pass in the street, walking in such pain and haste,
the color has drained from their faces. They are the foulest ghosts
alive, flinching from the intimate touch of morning air.
When I meet their eyes, they quickly look elsewhere.

No city claims me as its son. I've wandered instead
half a lifetime in slovenly forests and because of this am condemned.
I don't know my neighbors' names, who is their god
nor who is mine.

::

His daughter turned just that one time from the window
through which the light of her father's studio glowed
and all of her not-yet-conscious being saturated his–
a moment's glance. Three centuries later,

in the same city, a performance of a four-hour long trio
for piano, cello and flute, homage to a friend the composer betrayed.
They'd quarreled about figuration and the human form–
the grotesque canvases hanging there on the walls, listening.

::

It's only two day's train ride to the besieged city.
Unable to breathe in the empty coach, he closes his eyes
and panicking, tries to see that girl's face again in half-profile,
a precise and unambiguous oval of light,

the scent of oleanders, the memory of last things,
our sanctuary carved from darkness. The train to Nijmegen
approaches a bridge over the Rhine that tyrants marched
and retreated across twice in a hundred years.

::

She said she disliked that image of herself flushed with orgasm,
her naked shoulders leaning against bright whitewashed walls.
A strange expression on her face. Ill-at-ease in that city,
she wondered, *Should anything so frank be framed?*

Beneath the city 25,000 years ago, a hunter carved the intaglio
of an ibex on a cave wall and of himself drawing a bow.
The ashes of his fire, by whose light he drew, resist
oblivion–a black circle in the corner of the grotto.

::

At Rita's funeral, the Padre described heaven
as Disneyland! Mourners filed forward to take Communion
because–reversing the polar directions of our lives–
we're able to accept death only in the abstract.

How then shall bodies hoisted from wells saturate us?
Or the terror of a shrieking child caught in the crossfire of militias?
Or an entire nation stinking of rotted flesh?
At what point will the abstract no longer contradict the real?

::

In ditchwater.
The refugee road.
The ruined city it takes two days to reach by train.
Communion–the lowest form of vaudeville, art of the unspeakable.

A few pennies to taint a child's tongue.
The tyrant's face in profile on each coin.
A jittery young man leaves a package in the café.
In crowds, traffic, sewer-stench. Windows full of yellow dresses.

::

As Beatrice Martín danced, he ached with lust
for the elemental death she enacted on the dark stage.
Singer, guitarist, dumbfounded audience of middle-aged men–
in each of the dying, the green pulp of his bones awakened.

One man shouted out, *Olé!* because there is a variant of torment
so dire we understand our sins cannot be forgiven
by any formula, least of all by forgetting
we are lost, but no less dazzled.

FROM THE BOOK OF ESTHER

Purim comes around again, and a company of children
performs a political melodrama, fourth century B.C.E.,
in two acts: "Hamon's Treachery Against the Jews,"
and "The Triumph of Queen Esther."

With us tonight are two Esthers, one a visitor, a Gentile
friend of our host, and she watches and laughs, *gregor* in hand,
as the child who portrays her namesake asks favor
of good King Ahasuerus.

I wipe steam from the window. It is snowing in the city,
the twelfth day of Adar, the year poised at equinox.
All is as it should be. The air in this room sweet
with schmaltz, boiled parsnips, *knadlach.*

Queen Esther, pure of heart, always a girl crying out
to wear the crown forfeited by the royal concubine, her rival,
Vashti, who, dressed in black, we may presume was no fool
about the equation of power and sex,

Vashti, who refused the King's order to share herself
with guests at his party. And here, too, is loyal Mordecai,
Esther's kinsman, a chubby boy who forgets his lines,
whose mother coaches him in his role as eunuch,

keeper of the harem, that his cousin, Esther, will be chosen from.
But Esther, our guest, neither pretty nor lissome,
pursued another itch, both she and her daughter beside her
infected now, chosen for the early death.

What really are we celebrating? We were taught at *shul*
to read the Book of Esther as our twentieth century,
the Shoah, a metaphor of resistance:
never again.

Ahasuerus was no Hitler, but was actually Xeres, a fool
who whipped and fettered the sea, who sent away disobedient Vashti
in exchange for another whore, Esther; and Mordecai, the King's servant,
Esther's cousin, a pimp really,

simply outmaneuvered his own less ambitious rival, dim-witted Hamon.
Because of their intrigue, in Susa hundreds were slaughtered.
An ecstasy of bloodletting spread like a virus, scalded
the countryside and provincial towns.

The enmity between those two provocateurs, Hamon and Mordecai,
pretenders to the Grand Vizier, was very old, tribal, familial:
Benjaminites of the House of Saul avenging themselves
on the Amalekite clan, the Agags.

And Esther's legendary role? Allowing Agags to die
in our stead, denouncing a lecher, Hamon, who ended up
swinging from the gibbet he built for Jews.
That is what we are celebrating.

Betrayals bring us together in this aromatic room,
where the grown woman, the living Esther, remains,
no heroic abstraction, but dying–what we all fear, infected by
the shamelessness of our story.

AN OFFERING

Night of the Falling Stars, I dream of Old Oregon,
of a series of daguerreotypes in which the Columbia
seems an inviolate blur of dunes, rapids, standing waves
and in the background, northern forests, a smudged shadow,
a trail through the gorge disappearing into fog.

But when I wake on the fourth floor of Casita Ardilla,
the tiles beneath my bed are awash with morning light from Africa
and far below, along Calle de las Maitres, my neighbor
whistles to canaries as he stumbles home
from the finale of La Romaría.

Wherever I wished to go along that muddy path before dawn,
I was mourning a world already lost. Those men and women
in the foreground of the daguerreotypes, lifting their nets
from that undammed river, were no longer its subject.
Even before the flashpot burst into chemical light,

the moment vanished into the lush gorge behind them–
an oddly anterior future. After I dress and descend
the spiral labyrinth of the house, I unlatch the shutters
and look into the blinding street,
where inconsolable Antonia's face peers through wrought iron.

The ghost of the dictator haunting her misshaped body,
she reaches through the window across the flame of the hob,
demanding something of mine. Her open, upturned hand
every bit as immediate and appalling as you'd expect,
another way of knowing what has been will continue to be.

Into her palm I place the obligatory orange and today
also, a sweaty wedge of cheese.

FEST-SPIEL WEISE

A field outside of Nuremburg, the city
squatting in silhouette at the horizon. Black
towers, slate roofs of the ghetto. Sky above
pale and narrow. A scattering of clouds lit by
sun that is perpetually extinguishing itself
in the purity of the impure plains. Furrows
converge on a grove of lindens towards which
I hurry, a soiled gabardine tied at my waist
by the frayed rope I will hang myself with later.
A skift of ice, blue light of winter dusk, lies
in each trough of earth. And straw, golden straw
is strewn about the field. Not my daughter's
black hair, but fairy tale stalks the dwarf spun
into ore that dazzles our "dark, sad eyes."
Vanity in such abundance! Enough! Enough
to sicken a devil. O city of music,
the festival ground. Intimate as this black mud
frozen under straw, underfoot, under ice. Black,
medieval, twentieth-century mud. Ignorant mud
of the circumcised and the un-. Riches-at-harvest
mud. Shulamith mud. My daughter mud.
I offered her lips this dug of dry mud, "Please,"
I cried, "drink of me." It is our blood that stains
the sky. Ghosts through whose hollow gaze
you will always know a barren field. Gleaners,
nourished by blackened potatoes, moldy wheat.
Brazen and anxious as gray mice. Shadowy
tracks trailing us across the skift of dirty snow.

TEKMERION

Remind me, someone, it's only a matter of luck
whether famine inhabits a land or not
and infallible signs in no way prepare us for a rapture
that ruptures the small world.

If I go at dark to dump a bowl of Empire skins in compost
and a blue halo of ice circles the Hunter Moon,
how certain may I be that flocks of geese will form by noon
the next day, a cold rain arrive by dusk?

Bent over scythe and shears, on my knees by first light,
I cut stalks of annuals, shake out seeds,
fold perennials in protest of the coming freeze
that will outlast the night.

Let fools talk loudest who hunger for wildness,
I refuse, in October, to concede,
to unhouse my mind and choose
to hammer larch billets tighter in the woodpile.

A few geese squawk high above the garden,
gather into one flock, turn a last circle over the valley
and dive past Glass Hill, the customary V receding,
growing smaller in the south, just a dark filament in sooty sky.

Unhoused at last am I, spellbound by signs
or just the usual melancholy
of knowing we die sometimes before we die?
Or maybe I'm just stubborn?

Domestic provisions don't summon much confidence
nor does chopping away last summer's dry exuberances–
I make my prayers for the small world
to endure one more night.

And kneeling in the shelter of brittle leaves
at noon, I pick and greedily eat a few raspberries
tricked into late blossom and ripe
now, even as the canes rattle like death's hollow bones.

I practice my lost faith because, as I pack away the tools,
a frog peeps from its cranny in the rock wall
and all evening and all the next day
a mellow rain trickles in the gutters–

rain coming almost too late this year,
we feared it might not arrive at all,
the reservoir remain a mudflat valley of stumps,
the river a bed of algae-draped cobbles.

After the end of the world, if rains seem any less
random, I can't imagine myself
in this garden, a man, who–no smarter
or dumber than the rest, neither guilty

nor without guilt–sees rocket, kale and scarlet chard
unfolding from rotted straw in March
and fails to recognize these signs,
fails to feel unaccountably kind.

THE CARTOGRAPHER'S MELACHOLY

Traveling south between cities, he's trying
to read, but gets stuck on one sentence:
"Finally the journey leads to the city of Tamara."

And he remembers her as a young woman, Tamara,
twenty-five years ago,
they met one summer, friends of a friend,

her first months in exile. She'd bribed
border guards at the frontier,
after her city and its citizens became, not martyrs

but a sign for the capacity of people to act
with dignity and hope. All summer
he tried to seduce her, but each time they wrestled

in the dark, she pulled away and said sorry,
she couldn't. Soon, she left
to become an oil geologist, and he departed,

beginning an unremarkable life that led to this
train, this annotated history
of phantom capitals open on his lap, absorbed

in his sour regrets–not Tamara's absence,
but his own, how
melancholy and not a man occupies his seat.

On page thirteen, in blocky script in the margin
the first owner of his book wrote;
"We are residue of delinquent desires."

Past the glass of the air-conditioned coach,
sun bleaches basin and foothills
blonde as Tamara's hair that evening she said

she could no longer see him, apologized
and shut the door.
He walked to the corner, caught the Metro

a quarter century ago, then this commuter train
on which he feels poised again
at the verge of crossing from the dormant life

into a parallel geography, where expectancy
and phantoms permit us to live
multiple lives in concurrent times. By why?

Why bedazzle us with the invisible only to grind
to another frustrated stasis? What disappoints him
is the absurd calculus of fates, how their lives–

Tamara's and his, might coincide again, that,
for instance, tomorrow,
she will pass a café at noon as he twists lime into beer

and thinks something inane like citric acid
burns one's cuticles, they will glance as each other
blankly, then look away because this is stupid

fantasy, a middle-aged hypochondria, a weightless
existence in marginalia. Parenthetically:
"(None of us exist.)"

GNOSIS

She carried on about her failure too long. It leaned
precariously at the middle of the studio,
a rickety, reconstructed chest of drawers
high on a mound of mirrors she smashed,

her *Book of Revelations*.
Inside of it she had carved and painted
faces from the myth of her childhood. Not once,
she complained, because she knew the difference,

had the *Book* carried her beyond its mundane making,
a longed-for flight, the dissolution of self
by the grace of–

and here
she struggled for the proper word.

::

Another student, at the far end of the studio,
took a piece of charcoal in his left hand,
his right hand deformed, and began
sketching an ecstatic Jesus, the Savior's face

open as a child's, laughing at the follies of Thomas.
But in the corner of the paper, emptiness
demanded he bring it into being, a point of intimacy
where he must reveal the Son of God's right hand

reaching toward us, open and generous.
And fascinating to watch, like a striptease,
wondering, how far will it go?

Not far, of course.
With his grotesque hand he rubbed it all out.

::

We might have left that studio sooner, gone out
into the streets, joined other people heading home
after work, dissolving into snowy twilight
and soon, shared a drink, another night of forgetting.

I too have failed, forgetting
my own bafflement at the predicament
of bringing forth whatever is in us
before we destroy it

because of a flaw
that exists in the world, in ourselves,
so that it seems we are driven by ghosts,

by sheer ignorance and pretense,
destined to fail just shy of becoming
greater amplitudes of love.

OF WATER

There's neither two nor three.
Because the dying still wander from the blast zone.
Because you may "visit" where.
Because of the student.
Because of the city.
Because there's an island in the river, where.
Because the dying still lie in a grove of trees.
Because I don't know the names of the trees.
Because the trees, too, are a presence.
Because the student folds a chain of paper cranes.
Because in the photograph she points to.
Because of the sound of water.
Because they sing, "O, quickly, quickly now."
Because they sing.
Because the sky inhabits the skeletal dome.
Because they shave the collaborator's head.
Because she goes mad.
Because in the name of peace, the park, where.
Because *Himmel und Erde*.
Because, "Forgive me, I must pole your punt across."
Because she leaves origami cranes.
Because the dying raise their heads.
Because an invisible hand steadies them.
Because of the unreality of light, its apocalyptic absence.
Because we offer a drink.
"Of water?" "Of water, yes."
We bow. In gratitude and shame.

Departing by a Broken Gate

TO THE MORNING STAR

All month long, blue Saturn trailed
behind you and while he gazed
opposite your sun-lit crescent,
even sullen, pale Saturn
brightened in his distant house.
But he's swept past you now,
his reflected light like yours
dimming into daylight,
faint as a hermit's nervous fire.
So I've walked here earlier
each day along this cliff face
the hour before you vanish
into glare, and here, above town,
town's still obscured by fog
and I can hear only the clang
of disgruntled machines,
cold grease gliding reluctantly
into cogs. That's the sound
of people throwing away
the middle of their lives
as I'm throwing away mine
chasing money, telephones
humming with instant deals
and 10,000 lies we tell about
autonomy and shameless will.
It was better to waste
so many mornings walking here
with you in your dwindling light,
this shadow my body cast
on frosted grass, like all others,
rigid and fragile as glass.

ANOTHER METAPHYSICAL ERROR

Our teachers tried to explain it,
pouring out a mist of iron shavings
over a magnetized bar. "A model
of the invisible," they told us,

and then flipped the bar
one-hundred and eighty degrees.
Sudden disarray, charged particles
crawling like ants, one over the other,

a disturbed nest, until the pattern
reappeared: "Our way of knowing."
Face it, we'll always be gullible
as yeomen, gaping at the Hell's Mouth,

splashing watery ale all over ourselves.
Enthralled by a skein of tangibles,
our so-called Way of Knowing
is capable of expressing only

its preference for the particular,
here, now, the vehicle not the tenor
of what would otherwise seem
an inconceivable betrayal:

the reversal of poles occurs
so seldom, in time so expansive,
the story's been told only twice,
and then, only microscopically,

in realigned molecules of iron-clad
rock. We don't ignore it so much
as it ignores us, or is indifferent,
though we might acknowledge that

it's evidence of tribulation,
and for the righteous a winnowing,
a reward. Though it's no reward.
It's baleful and chaotic

beyond reckoning, when gravity lets go.
But for us, perhaps, not an unusual storm
of ions, but Heaven's spectacle:
four horsemen in raiment of gold,

there, galloping across the sky.

EARTHSTAR

I found one below a veil of water seeping from mossy ledges in the desert two years ago, an exotic flower, dried and bleached by sun, carried it home a thousand miles. In the library one day, I walked past a book lying open to a photograph of the same flower, only it's not a flower, it's a mushroom, the "inedible ally" of the puffball. One skin surrounds the spore sac, protecting the globe of microscopic seeds. The outer skin ruptures, divides into thin white rays that curl under the fruiting body, lift it as though on legs to hold the radiant white orb aloft, until one of the rays decides to reach back toward the center, as one must always decide, and depresses the tiny apical pore, the navel-in-reverse through which the cloud of being drifts out, a brief smudge suspended in air before it disperses in wind.

UNIFYING THEORY

Strange to see it again and feel the same disquiet as years ago. Limbs broken off one by one and burned to ash, just a few chunks of shiny charcoal in a ring of scorched stones. The decomposed trunk outlined by elk sedge. The crotch a spongy mound covered with slough of needles, bark chips, wolf bait. The rotten remains gradually thickening, turning from umber to russet near the root-clump, where a pile of worm-eaten particles light as balsa align along the axis of the grain. Such an orderly self-extinction! It seems now, as before, a deliberate, dignified act of acquiescence. There is no eternity inside of things. When I kick the drift of snow in the lee of the rotted tree, a young limber pine bent over and pined to the ground all winter springs back from the weight of snow retreating into shadows. But I still can't decide? A unified design? A random act?

ON FINDING A FRIEND DRUNK AT LOST LAKE

He must have lain here very still
on the forest floor where he fell

among puddles and leaves stripped
by storms. Narcotic fog that swept

off the lake between hemlocks and alders
must have concealed him from deer

who passed single file along this road
to the shore, where they bowed their faces

and drank from the dark, now
graying water, for they pressed dew-claws

and twin ovals of their hooves
right beside his face and that proves

even an unruly man can lie still enough
and forsake a disfigured part of himself

that couldn't otherwise hold its tongue,
curl up in the duff and be no one.

AFTER

The day the Exxon *Valdez* ran aground, spilling cargo and turning the flyway black with the oily sludge of commerce, we trespassed on the low, marshy reaches of Geckeler Slough, a spring storm pouring out of the "dragon's throat," columns of ash and debris swirling a mile along the dike from Hot Lake to the rookery, where eagles brooded in barren snags, swans flared and displayed, rafts of teals, pintails, mallards, and mergansers drifted over flooded fields, ten thousand voices as loud as wind that carried them north the night before. All that noisy, unruly exuberance–water breaking free of ice and rigid earth letting go its lush gasp–just another elegy. Every spring the world tries to reassemble itself, but there's always a part missing. It's April and the sky fills each dawn with migrating flocks, dropping to rest here as slow as ashes fall from a column of fire, the kingdom at the edge of their wings holding them steady in air we can only breathe.

THE MORNING CHORUS

The air rinses across the bodies
of lovers who lay half-awake, half-
listening at dawn in June. Stop here.
Don't go on. Or preface how,
in some cases, if you leave
an image out of context
it becomes a pretty lie of praise
for an unassailable innocence.
But engines already are intruding
on the amnesty of sleep,
the mercury-lit edges of cities
metastasize in the dark
and as for Beauty—what about it?
Besieged by indifference, Beauty
already has ceased to be anything
besides a privileged irony
at 4 a.m.,

when whip-poor-wills
quit their mournful whooping
and someone small—vireo, phoebe, chit—
whistled to its nearby mate and broke
the silence, thorny hedgerows
erupting, loud with multitudes of
thrushes and orioles, tanagers, towhees,
mockingbirds and jays, more than
you learned the names of, their pleasure
a vast wave of songs, not Babel
after the confusion of human tongues,
but a boundless accord passing from
one thicket to the next, calling earth
awake, north and south, teeming
tropics to teeming tundra, jubilation
at the miracle of oncoming sun.

GEORGIC: FOR MY FRIENDS WHO NEVER FIND ANY

Like the universe, that's how wild
mushrooms grow from forest mold:

everywhere is the center, find
one pitted cone and spiral outward

in concentric rings. By this method
you'll pick all the baskets you need

full of black morels, any morning
in May, when heart-leaf arnica

covers forest floor in unbroken green
that ripples like a pond when wind

tires of pinetops and comes down
to search modest things close to ground.

You'll need to squat a great deal,
pray to the mountain's god, who wheels

overhead, booming, pelting you with
sleet and hail. You'll need to sift

through the green shadow of orchids,
peer under the canopy of leaves nearest earth,

someone else's heaven, sky of a world
always underfoot, trampled, ignored,

very much like another world you know
better, but here, you will visit only

during a few weeks each spring, your giant
face like a rare planet in eccentric orbit.

That means you spiral, too, your life a ring
among a pattern of infinite other rings

with a random center of gravity.
Or there is no gravity

and you're one among many wanderers
wobbling blind in space, until that metaphor

evaporates like sleet and hail that melt
back into sun-lit air, and you just stand

here at the edge of a dark grove of firs
that didn't fall to chainsaws, and right here

at the margin between what was
destroyed and what wasn't,

you clap hands, laugh, and quickly kneel.

BEHOLD–THIS COMPOST

Incipient emerald, nest of earthworms, July jungle in which children will race and squeal like the joyful creatures they were born to be–this is the garden I smothered in compost, and that I stood by all winter, kicking at its edges, loosening a clod, turning over a damp mat of leaves to listen to the many languages spoken in its café of perpetual heat, where steam of rot rises, where shoots of chestnuts are delicate as a musician's fingers, and buried stems of Brussels sprouts form bundles of leaves like hands folded in prayer, where rags of sod struggle like Jesus, reversing direction, sending up pale yellow and passionate hair, celebrating the light returned from the south this blustery April day I've waited for, when I take a stride into the garden and shovel down in the volcanic soil, turning it over again, turning under russet leaves and whirlybirds that, on the first warm day, sprouted ten thousand maple seedlings! What else is there to do with a life as imperfectible as ours, where all that's alive is somebody else's food and what was alive is the soil from which it grew?

DEPARTING BY A BROKEN GATE

In low, perpetually twilit caverns and bogs in the canyon,
spent sedge, hellebore, aster, Solomon's seal bow
and bow again to earth until their flaccid stalks fold
and they collapse as they must in mother-mud,

to which, coming along this raised trail today, I also bow
to the earthbound, traces of early autumn,
puddles etched in ice, larches drizzling gold,
dust of first snow in long shadows of Douglas fir

and, seen through bare lashes of willow and alder,
vertigo of cliffsides, jets of water colliding,
lodging a complaint against unyielding stone–
be many   *be round*   *die.*

An omniscience, an odor of richness and birth,
rises from rotted leaves on the canyon floor,
rises from meadows, streamsides, split-rock crannies,
wherever long impenetrable earth grows soft,

darkens from drought-grey to black, opens,
becomes a bed of urgencies sown by storm-cast seeds,
this paradox without a name, though it soaks me through
with dampness of sympathy for things,

each equally aware, each articulating one verb,
an almost remembered sound, an agonized, long suppressed
grunt our ancestors heard their dying cousin Neanderthal utter,
though he couldn't explain it any better than he could meld

into another living kind–woman and man, you or me,
makers of tools, whose faces, like larches in autumn,
seemed to him lit by an internal lamp of celestial origin,
faces bewildered by that lonely sound he made,

his verb *to love*,
which meant in its most paradoxical inflection
to yield up a world
that does and does not end.

What Next, Old Knife?

//

AFTER HARVEST

If lovers part at dawn to hang all day
on the thornbush of torn wrists,
if bare beech woods on far hills
remain immobile as stone,
if crows rising with the sun
shatter ice from swaying ferns
or on the river, near a creosote plant,
swans float in a sheen of oil,
if a gray cat, yawning, arches its back
and claws the bark of a tree,
if houses turn imperturbable facades
inward, shuttered and still,
if it's the final lull, if it's mud
loosening its grip, an iron door
swinging on dry hinges, Old Knife,
and pigs grunting down the chute,
if it's abundance, obscene lethargy,
spoiled grain beginning to mold,
harvesters departing, and mounds
of sugar beets at the end of a field
glowing faintly as faces in corpse piles–
what next, Old Knife?

MY NATIONALITY [REDACTED]

She writes every [blank], return [blank] altered,
but always the same [blank] inside, hinting of
[blank], of catastrophe, the necessity to [blank].
Reading [blank], I'm as confused as when

I started to [blank] the marriage in my head,
rehearsing, coaxing my dear, reluctant [blank],
my ferocious [blank blank blank], stumbling
[blank] on the soggy [blank] and boiled cabbage.

I walked back to the flat to [blank] a tonic
of the actual, half-timbers [blank]ed in bull's blood,
the walls [blank]ing like bellows, [blank] houses
more [blank] than the [blank]s whose faces peered

through lace [blank]ing from carved lintels.
What's the half-life of the [blank] for loyalty?
Is it twice that of the isotope for [blank]?
She didn't [blank] her passport either.

And I can't [blank] that anymore—whether
it's [blank] come hither or is she feeling
[blank]? My [blank] Czarina, my haggard [blank].
If her daughters [blank] in the beds of [blank],

who the hell's to [blank] for that? Every [blank]
benumbed, elided, and [blank]. O, my dispirited
[blank], full of [blank] for our imperiled [blank],
please don't [blank] away from me now.

[Blank] me baby, here in front of the [blank],
remind me who played what [blank]
by Domenico [Blank] well enough to [blank]
the [blank] and win a medal for third [blank].

SWALLOW IT

Give it a good shake. Go on
disturb the neighborhood. Rattle
the gate and rusty key-lock.
Nobody goes in there anymore
without first asking permission.
And who do you think you are
to ask, Mr. Outlander?
Mr. Here-on-a-Temporary-Visa?
It's really no concern of yours,
that walled-off corner of graves,
tumbled stones, root-bound rows
of a Baroque city's 19th century
Jewish bourgeoisie, still held
on suspicion. Whoever watches
from behind lace curtains readies
a reasonable answer in case
you dare to ask why. You might
make a scene in the street, addled
by how they allow nature this
slow erasure under pines. Indecent
this haunting little tableau.
Don't you wish you could let it go,
relieve everyone of the past?
But when you think about
how memory keeps score,
and how they keep even
graves of Soviets soldiers tidy
just on the other side of the wall,
that's an insult, like votives
burning before the fascist Pieta.
And you have to admit it,
you're at fault, acting obstinate
as a child refusing to swallow,

though in the end, naturally,
you'll get hungry and eat
whatever you're served.
They know this. You have to
swallow it, and so you do.

WE'RE NOT GOOD AT THIS

That's Oleg on the sidewalk a block ahead,
both of us in a hurry. We're late
for our adult language course,

though we're making better progress
than traffic that's trying to hold on the hill
below the stoplight, burning clutches.

I know Oleg knows I'm back here.
He saw me then went stiff-necked
outside a butcher shop.

So he's only pretending and hopes
I am too, as he steps up the pace a notch
and breaks almost into a jog,

trying to get away before decorum
forces us to speak. And he really is
running now toward a sedan

pulled out of the line of traffic,
over the curb and onto the sidewalk,
its door ajar, and then

(this seems so improbable) Oleg turns
and gestures to *Hurry, Herr David,*
Kemal offers us ride in auto.

Squeezed into the backseat,
I'm blushing with comradeship,
somebody's friend, *Herr David,*

national origins obscure, reasons for
living here impossible to explain.
Our teacher sighs at moments like this

and understands better than anyone else
the futility of trying to help
adult learners whose incompetence

must be excused. We're stranded
without her now in traffic,
blurting out all at once everything

we can think to say
in three languages we don't share
and a fourth we mangle so badly

not a word of it makes sense.
And that's as it should be
because we're men after all,

we're not good at this
and even our best effort lapses into silence
sooner than we're comfortable with—

an inept, grinning, ear-to-ear
silence, a little demonic—this
linguistic dead end where we simply agree

to nod, shrug and sigh, relieved
when Kemal finally slips the clutch
and eases forward two blocks, signals

a right turn, glides another two blocks,
signals left, the silence so excruciating
when he parks behind the night school

we scatter like diverse species of birds
fleeing from a feeder
someone kindly fills each day,

whole flocks of us frightened by
shadows moving behind window glass
in bright rooms, where people live.

IN THE SPACE OF AN HOUR

Sunday dawn, as I pull up the blinds,
a man throws open the shutters across the courtyard
three flights up, in the opposite block of flats.

He's standing at the window,
bent over a pot and scrubbing at rings
of scorched mush he left overnight to soak.

On the concrete sill, he's placed a yellow
bottle of cleanser with a green cap,
the sign by which I know (waving hello)

it's scented with artificial citron
to mask the stale odor of last night's goulash
in a kitchen as cold as my own.

Ice fog interposes itself between us.
Nothing and no one else has stirred.
Pigeons keep to perches under eaves,

the bakery van hasn't arrived nor the first bus
lumbered roly-poly to the corner, pausing
with a fumy, apologetic sigh.

What calls us forth isn't triumphant.
It's not the tigress on TV
batting aside her cubs and lowering her face

into the ribs of a roebuck, it's not
a benzene laced river, it's not a pit
full of charred swine, nor a child's bronchial cough.

We live no larger than the distance
we can walk in an hour, whispering a vow
to shop windows, *I'll persist*

and with any luck, will not board
one of the trains that collide nor cross
the bridge destined to collapse, but will

go on immersed in the lexicon of the local
and all it secures. I may not see my neighbor
through the fog, but I trust he's up there

getting after it, *really scrubbing*, pausing only
to tip the pot toward the light, as though to inquire
higher up, where they're better able to judge.

I MISSED MY PARENTS TODAY

a drinking song

It always baffled me how they behaved
as if they'd never found a thorn inside
a loaf of bread, never cursed a butcher
for the filth he claimed was boar's collar.
After famine years, they sang like this
every autumn, arm-in-arm with friends.
As true for them then as for me now—
nothing at all disturbs. Not the queue
outside a latrine. Not the sulfurous
stench of the baths. Not even trombones
squawking in the town square. Yes,
I'd like another cup of wine, yes,
naturally, fortify it with a shot of schnapps.
Let the sun slip early under hills,
I won't complain. Let darkness clobber me
like a tall wave rolling out of the north.
Frost will spread its paralysis, filigree fields,
glaze the cobbles into hallucinatory swirls.
No one expects to be spared. We know,
birds returning south carry the grippe.
You won't hear any special pleading.
All exemptions denied. Winter is going to
prove whatever it has to prove
as I intend to spend what I provisioned,
giving away all I have left to give.
Of my God's wish for my happiness
I've little doubt. What greater happiness
than this festival? The cups continuing
to move, the booths continuing to sell.
Arm-in-arm in the passageway singing
verses that baffled me when I was a child.
And no reason now to break the spell.

YOM KIPPUR IN STUTTGART

For stained glass burning all day until dark. For the dark
and the breaking of our fast. For who survived. For reasons
more cruel than dying. For the privilege of becoming ruthless.
For having refused (or failed) to unlearn the lexicons of exile,
of cunning and guile. For the tongue that serves them now
that served their masters then. For this paranoid disaster.
For this bland concrete side street. For the security cameras
and the electronic gate, the guard with his holster and pistol,
the surrendering of passports. For this morning, this seat
among the *minyon*. For our bewilderment, these
differently paginated prayer books. For something going
a little out of kilter in our brains. For stone. For tablets
of stone. For imperatives carved into stone. For One
who lives inside of words. For One who is words alone
and silent as stone. For an old man who starts to shout
at a woman not his wife. For the men who try to calm
and lead him out. For all of the young, as yet undefiled
by death, filing out. For my being surprised by how many
already have risen and left. For the cantor on the *bema*.
For the mourner's prayer. For the litany of place names.
For the obscene utility of numbers rounded to the nearest
zero. For strangely intimate names. For my mind going
haywire, hearing again all those names. For the narrow
clerestory and the glory burning there still. For our wives
who glare from their seats in the balcony. For who have
known us in both sickness and in health. For the pensioner's
single room. For the hunchback of poverty. For the stubborn
and inexhaustible impudence of the living. For this city. This
Day of Atonement. This year 5766. For doors swinging open.
For children running again down the aisles to their fathers. For
laughter, the improbability of it. Undiminished, sixty years after.

CROSSING SYNAGOGENPLATZ

10 November 2005

Long after time scrapped its train,
the train we're on glides underground,
the engineer applying brakes
so we ease forward in our seats,
who always sped into the future,
losing momentum now. At every halt,
boredom disgorges passengers,
plenty enough of it for all of us
to have grown weary of the commute
from main station to end of the line.
The stairwells venting stale air,
the sticky handrails and depleted hope,
all of it, all of us, past and future,
emerge from a chrysalis of diesel fumes
and scatter down a dozen streets
leading away from the center,
where those long dead broke the glass
and set the fires that obliterated God.
Refrain ye, the Zohar advises, *from seeking*
for the thing that is hidden from thee.

What's hidden in the folly of blocks
of stone recovered from ruin,
ten lindens planted in honor of words
that called splendors from the void, vessels
ablaze with the radiance of the mind?
See ye any manner of similitude? Please,
dearest one, don't let them see you cry,
if you need to cry, cry only later,
otherwise you'll never find your way
to the end of this. Here be sorrows
numberless as those complicit with

the crime, drifting below us in layers
no one should disturb again. The glory
this world emerged from inhabited by
an absence grown so ordinary,
we take a shortcut through the center of it,
in transit to and from work, leaving tributes
of gravel on the gravestone of God.

ON EBENALP

On a balcony at the base of limestone bluffs,
where the belay pulled free and faith failed
stolid Bernd, age twenty-nine, on this ledge
seven years ago, his body leaking sparks
like a power cable chopped in two.
A new young couple has replaced him.
Their backs turned to Bernd's memorial plaque,
they sort through climbing gear
and survey routes up the fractured pitch.
I try to follow their gaze as high as I can go,
but earth and sky somersault inside my brain
and either I'll look away or tumble backward into space.

::

Standing up here on the face of Ebenalp
(*this penultimate morning of my fiftieth year*
is how I intended to begin this
muttering to myself), I admit believing in
a fuzzy, Romantic commonplace:
I'm drenched in the capital S
Sublime, the silver surface of humid air
reflecting sun, a living membrane
through whose pores we pass into the presence
of pure being, these glacier-polished Alps
glowing in divine light.

::

William Wordsworth crossed the Alps
in 1790, age twenty, the very moment
he discovered alpine scenery
and revolutionary zeal. Conflating the two

in his mind, he *clomb with eagerness*,
then outlived his youth and middle-age,
endured the sniggering contempt we reserve
for the irrelevant and old,
and by the end, chose a stoic's *fortitude,*
and patient cheer, and frequent sights
of what is to be bourne–
shipwreck, tumult, anger, rue.

::

I confess what I told the inventor,
Cavinetti, months ago,
before he shooed his daughter outside
and locked himself in the garage.
We stood side-by-side at a cocktail party,
Cavinetti so stinking drunk he offered
to sell me all the women in the room,
even the Second-Wave feminists.
I was gassing about the toilet scene
in *The Seventh Continent*,
how, preparing for their suicides,
the family withdraws
all the money from their bank account
and begins flushing fistfuls of Schillings
down the commode, a gesture
more appalling to audiences
than murder, as viewers objected
to the squandering of capital
but hardly murmured their dissent
when, in the rubble of their flat,
the parents botched their daughter's injection
and had to try again.

::

Gestural, sometimes even noble,
suicide concedes nothing
if not progress toward the goal
of history, like a bad actress
who accepts a public scolding
and promises to rehabilitate herself.
Or it's just a punchline, as in:
In a moment of unusual lucidity,
Aunt Lucy hanged herself.
But given Cavinetti's pride,
his money troubles, suggestibility,
and overall weakness of mind,
was I somehow goading him to do it?

::

At the funeral mass
the congregation struggled simply
to comprehend the oddly inflected
English of the young Kenyan priest
who began, *We must leave our faith*,
perhaps a provocative gambit,
though it resolved itself in the usual
circularity: *It is so because it is so.*
Our Lord, Crater Un-cratered.
From there, his rhetoric devolved
into a baffling denunciation of
Heidegger's and Buber's beak lice.
So whatever Cavinetti's reasons
for gassing himself in the garage,
his despair expired in farce.

::

Higher up the mountain, the eager
young couple who superseded Bernd
have ascended the fractured rock face
flawlessly, full of zeal, each move
exact and exhilarating,
and nothing yet they know of
tastes of gall in their throats.

::

Before descending the path
with cables drilled into stone,
I watch a man my age cutting hay
in pasture so steep, if he loses his footing,
he will slide off the edge and tumble
a thousand feet. It's no great quantity of hay
the man risks his life to cut–just enough
to fork into a trough this evening
when lunatic clanging of bells pauses,
and milk cows standing in stanchions
go dreamy-eyed with relief.

CARVED FROM THE PIT OF A DATE

Mapmakers superimposed one Jerusalem
upon another, until Jerusalem acquired
the necessary buoyancy to float free

of its disputed sovereignties, as we–
outside the walls, in stony hills, a grove
of cypress and palm, at the threshold

of another new world, midnight of the fifth
great day–extend our hands across barb wire
into the fold. It's not the moon rising

but a shimmering disc of swans swirling
on an axis, a thousand and one feeding
a thousand and one each from its own breast,

rising, receding, irrevocably into blue,
that word like air sobbing from
a bellows, *blue*, until it's my own voice

waking me in the dark under the tower,
cigarette smoke from the balcony next door
drifting through window and curtain,

silence, but for the heavy beads of rain
rolling off of leaves and tapping softly
on paving stones in the courtyard below.

Bewildered, my head in my hands now,
overwhelmed by the enormity of justice,
the lassitude of my waking life, rubble

of cities and whole peoples my nation
laid waste. It's strange how close that man,
whom I've never seen, stands by my bed

each day before he descends the stairs
to whatever work he finds in this city.
He must have heard what I cried out

in my sleep. He stubs out the butt, either
ashamed for both of us or pitying a fool,
and slides the door shut along its metal rail.

WORD OVER ALL, BEAUTIFUL AS SKY

Chagall windows, Mainz

The tall doors I thought bolted
gave way and swung with such
well-oiled ease, I lurched forward a step
and stunned, breathed a blue mild
as the arms that held the infant Tobias,
a blue that glows at the core of silver,
blue of comets at the zenith, blue glint
of armor angels wear on errands to earth.
In no way I could conceive of was that blue
a lie, a pretty delusion, a hoped-for answer
to the question we keep asking empty
space that never says anything in reply.
It was the divine itself, though I believe in
no such thing, besides the necessity of it
struggling toward us through the layers,
returning from its exile in the absolute
zero of the void, what is possible always
asserting its fidelity to this world,
full to its brim with sorrows. There,
high on the walls of chancel and nave
twice reduced to ruins by war, the blue
of reconciliation, *word over all, beautiful as sky*,
blue a man, no god, conceived of
in the final year of his life, an old man,
full to the brim with praise, despite
the farce that deformed entire peoples
and scattered us like pieces of broken bell.
That man, even as he fell into oblivion, fell
without a trace of regret, this radiance
pouring from his mind, blue we know
isn't suitable for shelter, isn't an angel
bearing good tidings to earth, nor armor
that can protect a mother or her child.

Folly

THEATER OF THE ABSURD

Take a tuft of mountain goat wool snagged on a shrub,
pinch it, roll it into a small oily ball.

Smudge coal dust on it for eyes, leave cavities
at either end, gravel for the intestines in-between.

Add vapor drifting across lake water at dawn.
Squeeze it in the middle to start it breathing.

The creature we'll call a man. Leave him alone,
and after a couple of thousand years check back.

It's the middle of his life, and he's trying out
naïve notions of spiritual hygiene and alpine scenery.

One night he wakes under stars, staring into space
dumbfounded by the improbability of being.

Arraying the heavens with billions of galaxies
receding toward oblivion is a game gods enjoy.

He lies in tranquil ruins on earth, trying to
calculate the odds, all the metaphors seeming

what they really are: absurd semblances, follies
in the Fun House. It's true the mirrors fooled him.

All along he thought of himself as taller
and slimmer than what he really is:

this mechanism, this instrument of gods,
this body and bad brains I say I am,

I am?

WHAT IS TENDERNESS ANYWAY?

In the barber's chair beside me, a feeble-minded woman, who usually stumbles through the streets hunchbacked beneath a sack of empty cans, lies with her huge head in a sink. Gail is washing her thin gray hair. The woman twitches her shoulders as water begins to trickle over her scalp, and when she speaks to Gail, she chirps, "Tickles, tickles, tickles." It's too intimate to watch–Gail's hands moving through that filthy matted hair–but I can't stop gaping at the two of them. Joelle, who is cutting my hair, places both her hands at my temples, straightens my head in the mirror, and scolds, but soon I turn to stare at that woman's unabashed, "Touch me, touch me." How does such frankness survive its infancy, that god-like child before the eclipse, before permanent shadow sweeps away brightness from our faces? Why not hers? Joelle eases me around to face the mirror. She's done a fine job again–short on the side, thinned on top, has run the delicious electric razor up and down the nape of my neck more times than necessary to shave away my hackles. But there, at the edge of the mirror, is a tenderness I keep failing to find in myself. Gail stands over the shivering woman, probes through her curls with soapy hands, lifts them outward from the skull, unbinds the tangled knots, and murmurs as she rinses warm water over the balding pate, "There you are, sweetheart. There you are."

MY BOULDER ISN'T

My boulder isn't a metaphysical problem, nor a metaphor of human passions, nor heavy griefs, nor the unconsciousness of the unitary executive branch of government. It isn't symbolic of what is old beyond human knowing, the fallen-to-earth energies of comets bombarding the early solar system, delivering essential minerals of life. It's just a boulder, a common example of Wolf Creek gabbro on whose exposed edge I bent the mower blade last fall, cutting down weeds in the vacant lot I call The Lawn. It's my boulder because no one disputes that claim, and I've chosen to dig it. Twice. At first I failed, believing I could lever it to light, roll it across the grass, set it in my garden, an object of obscure holiness, altar of futility, an ornament to appall my neighbors, who aren't inclined toward boulder worship. Now, a second time, I've dug a deeper hole, a nest for an imponderable fossil egg. Down here beneath the sod, the smell of pale hair-roots subsides in clay that smothers the old stream bed whose gravels I've just uncovered. Here's a place animals drank in the Pleistocene. Camels, four-toed horses, a mastodon, a giant beaver, a sad and soon-to-be-extinct Oregon rhino. I've dug up under the boulder so that it might decide to roll toward me and crush me like the shell of a crawdad is crushed by a bored child. My boulder is compliant, ready to please, resigned to depth. I dig beneath it again, and again it rolls where I desire, to the south now, beneath (at last!) the surface of The Lawn. Such a fine hole! Vaughn, the four-year-old neighbor affirms this, peering down at me, amazed, "Big hole, Dave!" My wife walks past with a basket of laundry and mutters something I can't hear. When George stops by, he encourages me to keep digging, "Not much farther now!"

LISTENING TO SHOSTAKOVICH

Later, it seems just plain stupid,
there's nothing sinister about the question
and the man who asks it over drinks
before a dinner party in the suburbs
isn't an informer, toying with you like a fly
before your arrest, he only wants to know,
hearing this painful, chaotic music,
would you prefer to be its composer,
one of its musicians or its audience?

Your manners aren't very good,
you think about it far too long
and start to get gloomy not glib,
which is all that the situation asks.
You're new in town, and afraid
that you're going to insult him,
you'll never be friends–so you make a joke,
misquoting Mandelstam to the effect
that all the elements of music exist
simultaneously, but he polishes off
his glass of pinot and recognizing you
as someone out of your class, says,
turning away for the rest of your lives,
"No, you envy the composer."

But listening to Shostakovich again
today, you're still trying to answer him,
knowing, at least, you prefer that no one
hurt the way violins–detaching themselves
from the gray and grieving water of viola and cello–
hurt you as they sweep like squalls across prairies,
kicking up swirls of grit and debris,
the particles of exile, that bit in the camp

when there is never enough food
to keep you from stealing
off the weaker prisoner's plate.
Each violent measure warns of the next:
a train stops along a siding, bored troops
unload saboteurs whose feet are wrapped in rags,
a hound traces the scent of escapees
who will be shot, flocks of young drakes stunt
and dive over a salt-ringed marsh, their wings
strain and roar as gravity eats away
at the sheer velocity holding this music aloft.

In the largo, you are trudging north
when an old spruce thuds across the trail,
and as you consider its cadaverous lethargy,
this alchemical riddle
for the transmutation of lead into light,
two girls, singing hymns in a boat far from shore,
answer in harmony, but there's nothing left in you
that's swift enough to hale this hallucination,
plead for them to hide or feed you,
nor do you feel any urge to charm them,
clown like a hungry comedian in a cabaret
the chaotic year before the tyrant is elected.

Why would anyone, even in polite company
and for the inane purpose of small talk
envy Shostakovich? Who would presume
there's something like celebrity or genius
in music that remains unheard
except inside its composer's stymied brain?
No thanks. Better decline that choice if you can.
Each of these notes is still crawling out from
under a pile of corpses, and you could
call that courage or madness
but nobody you know would volunteer for it.

The despair of these strings doesn't invite you
to dinner or out for a drink, the manuscripts
are buried in the garden, and only a fool
would want to know—in a recreational sort of way—
how this man's terror roiled with guilt,
having witnessed a certain fate
that for reasons he couldn't explain
he was spared.

A COLLEAGUE OF OURS AT THE INSTITUTE

A colleague of ours at the Institute for Advanced Numbing paused at mid-sentence and laughed, "I'm awfully sorry about this." Then she stumbled and fell, kept falling, even as we rushed to catch her body. Too late. Whatever was alive already vanished from the room, passed through brick walls, spiraled into a tornadic wind over the hills. That's the optimistic version, anyway. All week we mourn her, and, like the truly stoic gripers we are, we make a catalogue of complaints: ruptures, fevers, tumors, funguses on our feets, ravaged gall bladders with sour attendant belches–*aargh aargh aargh!* No one says what we really think, which is that so-and-so will get her office–after her bereaved relations clean out the desk and a decent period of time passes. My friend is so upset he shakes me by the shoulders until my head tips back and forth, as though I'm nodding, eager to agree. "Don't you get it? She was younger than we are!" He's right, I agree, it seems a little indecent, the way Death mocks us. It's like twenty-dollar bills were falling out of the trees, piling up in drifts by the door. We're too embarrassed to move. But Death keeps on encouraging us, "Oh, go on, help yourselves, there's plenty more where this came from."

AFTER *THE RECORDS OF A WEATHER-EXPOSED SKELETON*

Basho, as he begins his journey to his native village,
confronts an abandoned three-year-old boy

crying in the mud beside the Fuji River,
victim of "the irresistible will of Heaven."

He gives what food he has and departs
without so much as a word of regret,

"Child, you must raise your voice to Heaven,
and I must be on my way." But we hear only

hooves of Basho's pony splashing at the ford,
and that child–runt, bastard, hare-lip,

whatever its failure–that child just sits there,
gnawing abstractly on a rice cake.

I stop, close Basho's book. It's spring.
Everything in the room glows with dusty light–

pine bookcase, oval jades, geraniums,
even red pumice pocked with pores of darkness.

Because I've forgotten about it, each time
I read this passage, I catch myself dumbstruck.

Do I believe that child is the only one
ever to die like that, a rare event,

as if justice was the common bread we break,
and pity wasn't powerless? But what else to do?

Explore the deepest cave and bring back
the neglected mineral light of first love?

Begin a mission? Vote a straight ticket?
Give away a few comforts to the poor?

It wasn't spring that day along the Fuji River,
and no doubt Basho found little hope

in this lie people cherish most:
there's no shame that irresolute instant

we fold ourselves inward, assured our dying
won't be such lonely business after all.

Basho, a man my age, more disillusioned
about the inexorable outcome,

chose to leave that child behind in mud
with all the food he had left to give.

Three centuries pass and that boy is still
sitting there, crying in the mud, unappeased.

TITHE

Some apples remain always just out of reach
of three-legged ladders and our outstretched
hands, as in October, when yellow jackets growl
inside overripe fruit that never seems to fall,
no matter the wind. Russet globes hang in trees,
rusting, mushy, molding, but very sweet
under the skin, a drunken feast for those of us
who haven't forgotten our wings nor how
to fly. It's not really a generous concession,
a tenth part, though it's no less our boon when–
in the crowns of those trees in January,
sky low and bleak, nuthatch, waxwing, towhee,
and the loud, misanthropic jay, all hungry
vagrants of the snow, jabber as though at a Jubilee.

AFTER A FAST, IN A FIELD OF GERMINATED WHEAT

So much green, incipient wheat! I'm hungry now for all the bread I've ever eaten, and all the loaves yet to be proofed, raised, baked and gobbled up while still warm and steamy. I don't mean those gooey white slices that constipate aristocrats, but black, molasses-rich, democratic loaves torn open with comrades, thick chunks smeared with schmaltz or cream cheese, washed down with pints of beer. Beer is bread in one of its two liquid forms, the other being sourdough starter (stinking, fermented snot of mules, the pioneer's yeast of grim necessity), which, when stirred in its earthenware crock, bubbles up and sighs with gas. In each loaf, biscuit, or flapjack is the memory of immigration. And it's the immigrant's poverty and abandonment that are also the essential ingredients in matzos, the bread of affliction Bubbe let me gnaw to keep me quiet as an infant. O Bubbe, who smelled of rye bread, her flesh the scent of toasted caraway, who filled the entire house each dawn with an aroma of warm bread that asked, *What kind of prince is this, what lies in the bed while others work?* It's time to break the fast with a common loaf—fresh, flat, yeasted, or stale, it makes no difference to me, especially today, at the dim end of November, the snowline lowering from the ridges into the valley, brittle weeds scraping the wind's disenchantment. It's time to break the fast, as everything that's going to endure winter, turns inward, resolute as the wheat's taproots tendriling into rich volcanic ash. Ash that in dry months is dust. Ashes and dust, familiar sum of all our becomings. But at either end of these thousand-acre fields, mile-long rows of inch-high seedlings converge where the grain hopper turned, rows swirling together now like a mist of green foxfire, lovers at climax whose bodies diffuse into the other, the globe of vital spirit the master directs along a vast curve back to "the elixir chamber" below the lungs. How alive our bodies are! The ache is lasting and wonderful!

The Open Hand

//

DEDICATION

For you who struggled to speak
and succumbed to muteness,
who spalled the chips from flint
of wordlessness, who flared
then went dark. For you
in whose fields dampness rose
from furrows sun and wind
soon dried to dust. For you,
caught by the gravity of tides
and drowned tangled in kelp.
Who felt the maple bole gnarl
into a hymn to goat-faced gods
unperturbed in heaven. For you
who fired the communal oven
in the square for the last time.
Who *Knead us into God*, you sang
to vacant air, *Breathe us into dark*
bread that we may be infinite,
divided, in equal parts shared.
For all who found muteness
uninhabitable as ice-scoured
stone, as barren glacial milt,
snowfall without laughter
of children. Who cast off shoals
confident abundance glimmered
in gunmetal seas. Who stood
alone like the soloist at the end
of music, wailing into the bell,
querying air with wounds.
Who aspired always to a form
surpassing all other forms,
who, unwilling to yield, believed
in broken cries. You, who were

the refuse, error, and debitage
woven into the words of others.
Let us claim some healing now,
the possible amplitudes of awe
that come around only once
in a lifetime, if at all.

DREAM AT THE JAFFA GATE

Absent fifty-three years,
my father greeted me
just inside the barbican
gate to the Old City,
and handed me a satchel
full of laughter. He must have
known I took the old one
full of woes he left behind
to a saddle-maker for repairs.
Besides those few years
hurled at us like stones,
my father has remained
dead. This is the first time
he's returned to tender
an appeal. He is gentle
as bees foraging lavender
in July, the thrum of wings
and soft breeze they raise
against my cheek when
I lean close. Today, all day,
I will become the joy
inside his gift and lie
here in grass beneath
this infinity of blue.
There must be honey
stored away somewhere
inside the sugar ash
with all the mercies
granted lives.

IN THE CHURCH OF THE HOLY SEPULCHER

Centuries have not redeemed us
from commerce, disputes enough
to fill archives—receipts, claims
and counterclaims—the only evidence
we existed. So we kneel, full of rural
longing for displaced neighbors,
people who could not endure
the local sorrows, dullness of lives
lived in provinces never visited,
far from trade or pilgrimage routes.
Nothing there but fields, puddled
roads, fouled wells and moldy bread,
sick livestock. Our whole lifetime
misspent, bowing to the violent
insurgencies mustered by a priest,
the manor or oligarch, those living
in splendors unattainable as long
nights we dreamed of when young,
asleep in the arms of local beauty—
a cobbler's daughter with flaxen hair,
the baker's handsome son, a young
widow, the tinker, the winter traveler.

KINNEHORA

The Devil goes about his rounds in rags
dragging his lame foot,
pissing maelstroms of battery acid

and as Bubbe always used to warn my sister,
the Devil pulls lizards from his bag to drop
into the open mouths of sleeping girls.

That's our Adversary you hear now
in the next block, laughing
like a table saw cutting through boards,

and maybe that's him, too, in the flat
upstairs, slapping the child
or scolding a very bad dog.

Bubbe would spit over her left shoulder
and mutter the counter-hex,
kinnehora,

believing the word returned our world
to stasis, a standoff
so embarrassing to our creator

he withdrew from all of creation
and has remained absent ever since,
forcing us to improvise.

TRYING TO GRASP IT

Dusk brims up at the windowsill,
spills onto the floor, larch embers glow
behind the tempered glass of the wood stove
and a couple lies entangled on a burgundy-dyed rug,
the stereo rattling French doors.

It's impossible to ignore the dark
clot that has lodged itself inside the mezzo's breast,
as she nears the finale of Schumann's *lied*,
Ich kann's nich fassen, and like the singer
to whom "sorrow came naturally,"

the couple cannot grasp it either
in their Jaipur garden of woven wool,
nor can the pianist who is trying to
keep this blissful little death in sync,
accompanying them all on the same ecstatic wave.

The couple changes position, tempo,
fully concentrated on their grave syncopations,
forgetting the live recital over there
on the other side of the glass,
and when it all comes to rest,

it ends in silence—a gasp, and then applause,
intervalic bravos and huzzahs
filling up the little room
as the doomed beautiful singer bows,
dabbing blood from her lips with a linen hanky.

THE HAPPIEST DAY

The day I waited for all autumn
has ended and I have kissed
my son's cheeks on a platform
opposite the slower train
I must board to return to my flat
in Ludwigsburg, late tonight.
This day that began in fog,
this day I waited for all autumn
has ended, the fog dissipating
early, the air soft as the sheen
of a wet pearl. I looked forward
to this rendezvous with my son,
who has grown to manhood
and towers over me now
full of goodness. Together,
we passed cafés redolent with
coffee, the sound of pressurized steam
foaming stainless cups of milk,
and passed along the streets
crowded by the young or retired,
the married or courting,
others sharing a glass of wine
with friends they missed all week.
How happy everyone seemed
among the storehouse of riches
glistening in the market–*filderkraut*,
onions, muddy potatoes, leeks
and kale, blushed Boskoops
picked this morning and an old woman
recalling how she tended the trees
when both the orchard and she
were young. Children ran,

as children always do
and one tumbled and wailed,
his mother dashing to hold him
in her arms, swearing
the sight of his blood is not
the end nor the meaning of life
and all seemed forgotten,
the boy's face glowed again
in the buttery light of a bakery
she led him to the window of,
full of breads and creamy yolks
and everybody else shyly smiling
at one another because we waited
to taste this sweetest day, a day
to recall through all remaining days.
My son has boarded his train
and waves farewell, *tschüß, adieu*
to all that we have to wait
a lifetime to savor as we did today.

THE DISCIPLE

I didn't dare turn away from that crazy
man in the tiny storefront on Rue de Trévise.
He pointed two fingers at his blue eyes.
Miracles, he said, *the Rebbe, he sees miracles!*

His disciple, apparently, saw them, too,
worshipping even the genius of likenesses
and all else that people invent, mimicking
whatever is above, beneath, or in this world,

the graven acts God forbade–all of it dazzled
the Rebbe's spiritual eyes. His disciple shouted,
Close your eyes, you will see and I did as told,
in remembrance of sun, earth and moon,

the visible planets like colorful Kiffa beads
strung along the ecliptic, all phenomena
an infinitesimal mirror of the shattered
vessels of Godhead and I vowed to try

and see my beloved's smile so deeply
inside of me I could not bear to live
if I must depart this world without first
carving her image from heartwood of oak.

Let me polish this statue a thousand years,
until the opaque seed moans open
inside of me again, green shoot groping
from my groin toward dampness and heat,

because what wants to go on living must
speak through us–even the dead to whom
it's forbidden to speak, as it's forbidden
to listen to the psalms of lost souls.

The disciple said, *Rebbe said, honor what is*
passing before your eyes. So I honor this
winter light at noon, an interior room,
basin, jug, ladle, soup tureen, pewter spoon,

caravans trading indigo-dyed cloth from
Chungdu to Istanbul, the stars, the spheres,
the chazzan's holy song woven from
wonderment, spotted cattle, half-wild sheep

and soap bubbles, whistles, rattles, a laughing
plaster clown into whose mouth children toss
hazelnuts. These be the prizes of eternity.
An infant crying, a mother opening her gown.

Ocean, pale wave, this monochromatic line,
this numinous curve rolling softly up
the long beach toward me, becoming
my beloved's nakedness waking at dawn.

ON COUNTING TO INFINITY

We were picking grapes above the Enz
and somebody in a nearby row told an old story
about a village boy who was a little slow
and how his teacher convinced him
to count toward infinity—that,
the boy reckoned, might take all year!
The teacher, for his part, warned
who can predict if it ever ends?

One night the boy saw a couple naked
behind a hedgerow and got caught watching.
Later, he mustered with others
and marched to the Western Front.
Returning, the war had subtracted
from his leg below the knee.
He spent the interregnum divided
against himself, a fraction of a man.

After another war, the village rose
from ruins and he joined in cleaning up
the labor camp, sorting bodies from trenches
into which they threw dissidents—
Catholics, Norwegians, and Danes—
and a few Jews, who needed to be
re-numbered before re-interment
in the memorial nobody wanted.

That started him counting again,
refurbishing Roman terraces
from rubble, countless limestones
lifted into place, a task three kilometers long
and high as the valley is deep. He quit,
age 93, claiming he was closer now,

having replanted these vineyards
to aid in happiness and forgetting.

But nobody forgets in a village
and everybody still laughed about that
evening he got caught behind a shrub–
he liked to watch!–staring in frank wonder
at the wonder of a naked boy
lying between a girl's legs.
"Are there any more numbers after that,"
his teacher asked. It took a lifetime
to answer not only if, but reasons why not.

SAINT JEROME RIDES THE T

Our lives unraveling in rain, late Sunday
in March on the platform, when we hug
and wave goodbye to sons reared
to manhood, who turn away and disappear,
reminding us of the shame of knowing
we are redundant and crude, perhaps even
a little deranged. Paula, forgive me
for my constant complaint. In a painting
your saint prays in the wilderness of Phrygia,
after the days of miracles already had passed
and would never be restored. The groves
would never again teem with crowds,
the cured, the healed, voices of children
at play. It seemed so brief, that moment
fulfilled even as it broke my heart. A stone
in my fist, I pound my chest, the lion inside
my clouds of doubt, the sagging flesh
upon its crooked timbers. I never grasped
the erotic, though you urged, baring
your shoulders, your thighs, the deep
curving hollow of your back, long hair
unbound. Paula, dearest one, I cannot
undo my vows to solitude, this umber murk,
underworld our grim maker rendered
with few scumbled brushstrokes, the tiny
confines of nature, and no anti-nature
gleaming beyond its border. We count
each station as it passes–seven more stops
to terminus. And seal our tongues tight
against the roofs of our mouths, trying
to stifle what we know is already lost
and therefore becoming words,
impure always, wayward, confused
and mistranslated by every generation.

AT YAD VASHEM

So as to keep a place to return,
these strips of A4 paper cut thin,
bookmarks on which someone wrote
given and surnames, on which he,
visiting from far away, scrawled
in flowing European script–
Alfred Anna Walter Wolf–
names often in fragments now–
rie dine schin ude rab er ah–
cut off again, cut in half, names–
him Herschlik ech osberg–
misspelled, names only heard
spoken by the old to the young–
enberg dor rzimmer x Froyda–
and never written down by the young,
old now, who fill the chairs
in this room, this broad blue sky,
this winter day, sunny in the hills
above a young forest planted
in remembrance of the righteous,
trying to restore lives of the lost,
the left behind and murdered–
nheim Lilli er el al gang–
relics, traces, residue, shreds,
the failure of song–
Betti Siegfried Metta nhard–
but also the necessity of trying
to sing its broken words.

KADDISH FOR NICHOLAS MEER

May and July, the Dog Days
and now this dry October
among the tribal stones,
so many of us lying here–
Auslander, Radetsky,
Benjamin, Goodman, Weil–
three thousand and thirty
in all and as of today,
refugees from places
they were unwelcome
in our time and before,
plus you–youngest-most-gentle,
three thousand and thirty-one–
whom He maketh lie down
in henbit and bitter cress
alongside the Highland Canal
and constant hiss of mid-day
traffic on Alemeda, mourning
doves whinnying softly
between the limbs of ashes.

When we strewed your body
with dust from Jerusalem,
we had meant to go on,
our business being among
the living only–braiding
the hair of a girl, holding
the hand of a newborn, meals
gathered from gardens, served
to friends, the water, wine
and all that is ordinary
commerce passing between
abysses we call sleep.

What duty of ours here,
where only a few dead
are honored to excess?

Firstborn, what honor remains
besides our pile of pebbles
left here these six months
on an unmarked grave?
Your name–
what did it mean to anyone?
The old may remember,
but the young are gone
ahead and do not look back.
Your mother on her knees
presses her hand down hard,
because surely earth will give way
beneath her and you reemerge
healed by your journey
through dimmest Sheol. She would
speak if she could, if anything
besides rue would answer.
Something else awaits us
beyond you, but what it is
or where and when it begins
we are yet to learn.

THE PRIVATE LIFE OF DEBRIS

We sat shoulder to shoulder in the forest,
brushing away debris—
the cast-offs, the derelict and bereft

clinging to the concave caps and false gills
of chanterelles we picked in day-long
twilight pooled under spruce and fir.

The refuse piled up between us
on that flat stone—yellow cottonwood leaves,
red maple, ninebark, threads of horsehair

lichen, pine needles, and kinnikinnick,
desiccated whortleberries, and spider mites.

That solitude was all I wished to abide by
and live inside of with her,
that moment aglow with October sun,

the mud frozen in the trail packhorses
passed along overburdened
and wary, their driver unaware of us

sitting nearby, under the trees.
And the quiet just beyond the moment—

a slow accretion of slough drifting down
from the canopy over 10,000 years to settle
into our hair, onto our clothes, and our lives,

as negligible as any,
whether we deserve them or not
and for the time being only.

We carried our bounty home, our baskets
heavy the whole way, passing over
the surface of things, unnoticed,

into sunlight and out.

JULAFTON

The arctic night towering like a wall
in the starlit north, there I was,
stranded at a trailhead, forsaken,
pacing back and forth, trying my best
to stay warm, checking my watch
dumfounded by Skrymir's trickery,
sure the bus would soon return.

The new moon slid off
the edge of the earth. Dusk deepened
in the valley below. The cold,
as they say here, started *to sour*.
And from snow-blasted pines,
a man glided slowly as in a dream
down the trail and stopped to ask,

"Why in the world are you waiting
out here in the cold? This night
of all nights, shouldn't you be
inside with the ones who love you?"
I might have asked him the same,
though of course he knew why
and offered a ride to town, bound,

he said, by a pledge to do as a man
did for him long ago in a blizzard
in the Alps. Right then I was so cold,
I felt myself start to cry for the gift
that keeps changing hands,
making its private avowals
in the dark. Tucked in now

high under eaves, among the ones
who love me, I know someone else
stands out there still in the cold,
full of eye-shine and turmoil.
May the one who waits for rescue
also hear a stranger singing
the oldest song the world knows,

its melody decoded from cuneiform,
a human voice so full of welcome
hearing it we shed landslides of grief.
There's a bed for you, too, at the inn,
the old song goes, though nothing
warrants when, nor even if anyone
will place the gift into your open hand.

LINES COMPOSED ON JAFFA ROAD

My love's hair is molten waves of light,
that's what he says, that's what
bolsters him, passing through Jaffa Gate.
It's vermilion-gold cascades of harvest wheat,
and just the thought nourishes him,
calms his mind, her long hair plunging
in glory countless times before his eyes
when he held her shoulders in his hands,
jolted awake by a voltaic presence
surging across generations of exodus,
from one land to another. He follows her
until she stops and turns, her eyes' blue
fixing him in a stare that is like peering
into portals of sky, into all of human time,
all the years that will pass, the decades
determined to cripple, blind and drive them
apart. Just reminded of that, he feels
like an wounded animal, snapping at
phantoms who menace him, inconsolable,
wild with grief, an eternal absence opening
its chasm between life in their bodies

and desolation beyond life, *the loneliness*
on this earth without her. And this causes
every step he takes crossing this city
at dusk in the month of Kislev to tremble
under his soles. He hurries toward her
in a bleak little room they let, she bathed
and groomed and scented by rosemary.
It's the only solace a man ever knows
in this life or any other should he be
so fortunate as to love one woman
and rush to her side through streets.

All along the way, grates rattle up
in front of shops, there is the savory scent
of sautéed vegetables and lamb, shrieks
and laughter of children playing tag
outside derelict flats—all the young
and old alike are resisting the end of this
warm, generous day. Everyone is trying
to prolong the spirit of a Sabbath ending,
trying to forestall night with another sip
from the sweet milk of intimacy and rest.

WHAT SIMONETTA SAID

If you are the foreign stranger trapped
inside the excellent machinery
humming at the core of opulent nations,
you will probably be feeling like a rube
just about now, a pantaloon or clown
arrayed in your out-of-style clothes,
another irregular humorist
plunging blind along a network
of gantries, sidings and switches,
arriving and departing from stations,
always on time, but always worried
or confused, incapable of figuring out
the odd signage, the local routine,
a language that sounds ugly
in the mouth as knuckle bones
dogs growl over and gnaw until
they crack through to the marrow.
You will repeat in a whisper numbers,
the schwa-ed word for main station,
trying to pronounce the city's name
and this repeating it aloud allows
for some protection against error,
perhaps even a little confidence,
a conjuring of guidance, a good sign.

For Simonetta, the human heart
will be that sign and it will always be
a warm July night, wooded hillsides
and grassy meadows, you will walk
among thoughtful, generous people
and there will be music in a church,
a path through orchards and vineyards
lit by fireflies and truth will stand naked,

but never stand apart or falsely accused.
The baby who lies on the pavement
strewn with straw will light the faces
of three girls who kneel over him,
rapt by their sister's covert life.
What you have whispered to yourself
crossing borders, arriving in
or departing cities, will be the charm,
the shibboleth, the signal that destiny
means for you to exit here and board
the next train to the farthest suburb,
whose name, even if you mangle it,
becomes a song about first cousins
who will be waiting to keep a rendezvous
in a crowd of anxiety and hope.

The train emerges from dankness
into fields full of melons and flowers,
there is a smiling face waiting there,
holding forth a plate of Pecorino
drizzled with acacia honey,
somebody else is uncorking a bottle
and Simonetta is saying the only words
she knows of your native tongue
and that someone said to her once
and she never forgot the goodness of it
though she had to look them up
in a pocket dictionary to be sure,
but now she is certain and has rehearsed
all day what she wants you to hear:

Stay, enjoy.

Years Beyond the River

BALK

—before you fulfill
the performance of not being

these pasqueflowers and beargrass
radiant in the forest at dusk,

a lit face nearby
in shadows at the trailhead

saying into her phone,
the pressure to not be

in one place at the same time,
the gist of it being

lives splinter
or the waiting to admit it

is over

::

as when they called your name

and said to come inside
at the end of a spring day

to rehearse again
your sister's not being,

though by then you knew
to linger and not obey,

just listening as the contralto next door
sang lyric scales

at the open window,
enchanting and filling the garden

inside of you

::

where she falters still

in the lowest octave,
helpless as you are now

in the performance of not being
two mergansers

flying fifty-five miles an hour
along the river,

of not being hillsides
covered in balsamroot and cous

damp with melting snow,
gleaming as mottled sun departs,

the light mineral and clear.

AT THE WELLHEAD

There was going to be
a world of increase and jubilee,
prolific shade, afternoons
full of exponential ease
beside a stream and trout
skittering away like faces
erased from the final
measures of a dream.
We all waited for that,
even the dead,
who puzzled over sigils
scored into stones
someone, forgotten now,
raised at a crossroads long ago.

There was going to be
justice, the unity of one
and the infinity of June,
irrigation wheels in grain fields
singing work songs,
their casual *ch-ch-ch*
and a silver mist
risen from the steadfast
darkness inside Earth
would drench the skift
of emergent wheat
and us, too,
the partisans of these
manifold and bumper yields.

THE MUSIC OUR SON DREAMED OF

After the solstice, friable light
withdrew and scattered.
Ice fog veiled the hogbacks
and depths of field receded.

So who could say then
if a durable world or fleeting one
remained afloat
in blue ranging violet to white?

Our son heard his music's pulse
in those long twilights and soft
whir of seeds
from the crowns of firs,

in the red fox's breath
inside its lair, the muffled
thump a flying squirrel makes
landing at the mouth of its den.

He heard it resolve
into a chord as wind
sifted through pines,
then decayed to silence.

We heard it, too, at the New Year
in the way people resolved
to try and speak again
with magnitude, saying farewell

each time as if it were the last.
At dinner tonight, a child asked
would she remember the future?
The music our son dreamed of

answered the way a grouse
after taking flight
leaves the shape of itself
pressed into snow.

APOSTLES OF IMMINENCE

We sometimes meet people
who don't want to live
in the present.

In their darned sweaters, patched trousers,
long hair lifting in wind,

they seem startled
when we happen upon them
in the forest, bogged down
along twenty miles of drifted road.

Their wagon minus its wheels,
the woman holds the team
of sway-backed horses

as her man repacks axle bearings
in muskrat grease.

They have grown pale
with self-reliance and want
to re-litigate the past, argue history.

They are full of praise for hand-forged nails,
the striking of moveable type
and lathing of hames.

Though for them hope went extinct,
a feathered thing, circa 1970.

And now, stranded in latter days,
they bear the melancholy burden of the past
and warn us, there is a future
only they, drilled in privation, can abide.

For the time being though,
should we help to pull them free,
they will barter with us–

goat cheese wrapped in oil cloth?
wild honeycomb?
a pint of bitters?

AS THE MOUNTAIN DREAMS IT

There it is.
A glimpse of it anyway,
rising above the intervening ridge.

The dome of Glacier Peak
and headwaters of five rivers
we live alongside of

in all our feckless shambles and uproar,
Johnnies-come-lately,
ghosts of a language never learned.

At dusk, the mountain divides
shadows cast by its north-facing cirque
from alpenglow lifting along its southwest flank.

There it is. The world
as the mountain dreams it,
going on after as it went on before us–

spikes of elk sedge and calf brain
poking through duff at the edge of July snowbanks,
a whitebark pinenut splitting its seed coat

centuries later inside a nutcracker's hoard,
the fascicles unfurling five elegant seed-leaves,
a little asterisk on a mountain that lost its glacier.

If people live inside some spectral order,
does it matter how
or how long we abide here?

Does whatever the mountain dreams end
without us,
if it wakes in a world we set afire?

LATE AUGUST IN THE OKANAGAN

In the wake of the fire front
the stench of ashes
and skeletal pines. Teenage boys

sit inside an idling sedan
at the gas station
and can't believe their luck–

a Colville girl,
who, though she puts on
a hard brave face,

cannot refuse. She stares
straight ahead at steers
and ponies, seared obscenities

lying on their sides bloated,
dotting paddocks
and pretends she is

merciless. We belong
to no other family
and this idea of ourselves inside

a fireproof house. Think of us
sitting here as fire sweeps through
cheatgrass, as bitterbrush

explodes, the heat turned back
by mud walls and tempered glass.
Think of this world

that caught fire, each of us crazy
to open the door
and throw ourselves into flames.

A MESSAGE PASSED BETWEEN TWILIGHTS

It's years since we carried home the river cobble
from the mountain pass horse thieves
drove herds through to graze
at the headwaters of the Minam–
a cloudy violet quartz

polished by a river the cobble is
the sole evidence of, the time before
people fell into this world
and this mountain ridge
lay at the western shore of a continent.

Climbing there again today,
we followed a set of wolf tracks
in the snow above Squaw Creek,
brooded on broken forests and what
if anything, those trees remembered of her–

whose name, what tribe, which languages,
how many Julys gathered in her
and how long ago?–before violence
befell her and maps belittled
another woman and the place she lived.

The air so still in their battered stubs
we could guess which few
ponderosas and firs alive now
were young then, the creek resounding
in their creviced bark–the lyric

water sings even now in the cold,
splashing over every cobble in its bed
the same for us as for her. The mountain

gleamed, the sun warmed our backs
and we shared our meal in the meadow.

After so many years, that cobble
seemed to glow in its room
tonight among the orchids, a message
passed along tangled networks
branching to their thinnest mesh.

FROM *THE FIELD GUIDE TO NORTH AMERICAN MONKEYS*

Simia dolor borealis. Rare across its range. Prefers highland forest near open water. Matrilineal. Not gregarious. Forms loose-knit groups only when young are present, otherwise solitary. Retreats to isolated refuges in mature trees. Browses on mistletoe, clubmoss, horsetail, lungwort and blueberries where available. Needles of hemlock and red cedar fronds provide important winter forage. Individuals have been observed taking salamanders and tree frogs (*Grieve*, 1949). Often mistaken for juvenile Sasquatch. Typically silent, though, when mating, copulatory vocalizations sound imitative of and sometimes are confused with the melancholy yodels and harsh howls of others with whom it shares its diminishing range.

THE NORTHERN SORROW MONKEY

We heard it howl from the beach below
and moments later another answered
from krummholz high on the moonlit ridge above.

The moon-path led away
down the glassy lake to falls
we planned to portage days later.

Hemlocks in solemn robes
stood around us, attentive as we were,
startled awake and afraid of those daunted cries.

And we remembered a song, a round
first learned in kindergarten,
no, not now, not for you–probably never.

The Sorrow Monkey brooding
in its dwindled sliver of life, crowded out
by refugees from a world on fire.

Nothing else is possible
beyond the already-known–
there will be no adventuring forth.

Only hammering back into the familiar hole,
no achievement, no Infinite Theorem
or Hundredth Monkey, limits only.

The falls are the border never dared
and the range of its roar cascading over cliffs,
the moonlit dome of mist,

rapids churning below—all remind how
the farther a Sorrow Monkey roves
the louder the overawing rebuke.

FROM LATE JANUARY

A woman dressed as a bird impersonating a man
perched in the fire-galled pine
early this morning, near the creek.
By noon, a lens of ice
spun in an eddy below the hot spring.
Steam and a thickening green
poured through ice jams at every bend.
Not everyone we met in the mountains today
seemed happy, though some laughed
with the same affection we felt for a raven
who'd sought out people and waited at the cabin door.

It's just a bird, the woman said, *but still*
and the raven hopped across the threshold,
let her clean and reset its dislocated wing.
She held the raven in her lap
and the bird grew calm enough to sleep.
At twilight, we lay naked, listening
to the raven breathe
in its far corner of a snow-lit room.

CROSSING INTO THE DEEP NORTH

The first time my sister faced the nothingness of the sea,
she pulled me close and vowed to swim.

Her mind is so smooth with ferocity, she distrusts all maps
but for the inscrutable one unfolding before her.

And there she goes on skis into snowy pines at dusk,
this privacy we learned about after internment.

In a small town just over the border,
a woman watched as my sister fretted over denominations of coins

and pointed to the correct fare for two in my upturned palm.
We heard a recital on the radio one night and my sister

wondered why the pianist played a pulse of dark chords,
Is only one hand so full of grief?

In this country they say we are asleep in our outer selves,
but my sister is teaching me to be brave and jump, *I'll catch you.*

We've travelled as far as everyone else with wings–
the morning chorus reaching deeper everyday into the north.

And there is my sister again, treading water
below the diving board I'm shivering at the end of.

In the blue light at the natatorium
I feel sometimes afraid, but I love my sister.

It's almost spring where we came from.
Here too we sometimes can smell the ocean in the wind.

WE'RE STANDING ON THE GREEN LINE

when a fine rain falls the length of Meadow Creek–

porous, scattering blue,
everything in five dimensions
dissolves into it–

sedges and bunchgrass, us, the marsh wren's song,
yellow violets and cinquefoils,
the pink hair of prairie smoke opening at our feet–

my friend's voice nearby
urges dogwoods to hold the creek bank in place–

heal the skin of the small world torn open
centuries ago, its people murdered
or driven away, returning now–

it takes that long for violence to end,
for a scent this sweet and damp to guide us
back to what's steadfast
even in its half-year absence–

the lost and dear tremble awake
like a bumblebee nest beneath our feet–

our life aboard this rotting boat
someone long ago scuttled near shore
has grown new masts fore and aft–

and we're sailing into a green mist
filled with the heat of the hive
and glimmering with the wings of bees.

AT NINE-GEESE-CROSSED-THE-SUN

Since we last walked this ridge
with our infant son,
half of a lifetime passed.
We'd just said goodbye then
to friends we didn't know
we'd never see again,
and now, wherever our line of sight ends,
we re-stack cairns, dust them
with rotted heartwood of fir.

Remember us, we mutter
to paintbrush, to lupine,
to exuberant ninebark and mountain foam,
to whatever language is
the light it reflects–resilience-blue,
that's our favorite, pick-the-red-and-thunder
was our son's birth color,
rush-green is milk and sun
soaked up by its cream.

We didn't live the lives we meant to either.

LASTNESS

The first word lived inside
of everything then, a buoyant
music we roused to touch
the porous surfaces of

and it's rising through us again,
gathering flecks of clay
from the bottoms of wells,
gravity drenching us in a twilit room.

Acrobatic vowels warble
across a child's tongue, answering
another child, lost to us now,
who tasted honey from that hive.

Our faces bestirred
by the old quarrels in Sheol,
we don't want to forget last things–
the station crowded everyday

with departures. Lifetimes
a thousand deep trail us,
little bits of ourselves
sloughed in rooms, farm fields,

the villages left behind,
and snowbound forests
under whose canopies we sheltered
with migrants, runaways, unmoored men.

And here we are, besotted again
at this blue hour, your hair falling red
all around us, the held and beheld
in this storm of last things.

ACKNOWLEDGEMENTS

//

I would to thank the editors of the following publications in which these selections from *New Poems* first appeared:

American Poetry Journal: "Simplicissimus"
Cascadia: "Letter to His Ex from Fishtown," under the title, "After Spokane"
Chariton Review: "A Plea to Strangers"
Cloudbank: "A Blank Day," "Tzadik Moshe"
Coe Review: "The Woe There Is in Marriage"
December: "To the Angel of Forgetting"
Image: "When the Middle Game Is Over"
Oregon Center for Experimental Landscapes and Language
Innovation: "The Spring Classics"
Samsara: "Peripheries"
Saltfront: "The Readiness Is All"
Sky Island: "Below Medicine Bow Peak"
2 River View: "Along the Troll Løypa"
Under a Warm Green Linden: "Song of Extinctions"
Weber: The Contemporary West: "First Night Out Since You Died"

Other selected works are gleaned from the following collections:

Jerusalem of Grass, Ahsahta Press, 1992.
The Kingdom at Hand, Ice River Press, 1993.
The Chronicles of the Withering State, Ice River Press, 2004.
The Cartographer's Melancholy, Eastern Washington University Press, 2005; and later reprinted by Lynx House Press, 2018.
Departing by a Broken Gate, WordCraft of Oregon, 2010.
What Next, Old Knife? Lost Horse Press, 2012.
Folly, Lost Horse Press, 2014.

The Open Hand, Lost Horse Press, 2017.
Years Beyond the River, Terrapin Books, 2021.

Thank you to my teachers: Carol Kuhaneck, Barbara Armitage, Susan Weaver, Richard Hugo, Hank Harrington, Patricia Goedicke, Paul Nelson and Hollis Summers.

Thank you to the editors and publishers, as well as the artists and musicians, who supported the work selected here: Orvis Burmaster, David Memmott, Douglas Anderson, John McKinnon, Kasey Keeler, Kristin Summers, Mel McCudden, John Frame, Catherine Earle, Christine Holbert, Trey Hill, and Diane Lockward for the contributions you made to each of these books.

Thank you, Judd & Kathy Koehn, Peter & Loni Dines, Peter Fenn & Daniela Arcularius, Jan Hollm, Hartmut & Margot Melenk, Christoph & Heide Brudi for your kindness and generosity as I wrote *What Next, Old Knife?* and *The Open Hand*.

And may blessings always follow you, dear friends: Ola Fortner, Christopher Howell, Richard Robbins, Melissa Kwasny, Sandra Alcosser, Barry Kitterman, Piotr Florczyk, Jennifer Oakes, Debra Earling, Robert Stubblefield, Kerri Rosenstein, Noah Davis, Nikea Urlich, James Crews, Brad Peacock, Greg Rawlins, and the congress of democratic fellas named Mac in Lower Alliance, Ohio.

DAVID AXELROD teaches letterpress printing at the University of Montana on a 1935 Hacker Test Press and founded Bear Scratch Press. In addition to the volumes selected from here, Axelrod has published two collections of personal essays, most recently, *The Eclipse I Call Father*. He lives on former gravel pit where he looks after a small native plant nursery.